Artificial Intelligence Design and Solution for Risk and Security

Other books by Archie Addo published by Business Expert Press

Artificial Intelligence for Risk Management
ISBN: 9781949443516
https://www.businessexpertpress.com/books/artificial-intelligence-for-risk-management/

Artificial Intelligence for Security
ISBN: 9781951527266
https://www.businessexpertpress.com/books/artificial-intelligence-for-security/

Artificial Intelligence Design and Solution for Risk and Security

Archie Addo, Srini Centhala, and
Muthu Shanmugam

BEP

BUSINESS EXPERT PRESS

Leader in applied, concise business books

First published in 2020 by
Business Expert Press, LLC
222 East 46th Street, New York, NY 10017
www.businessexpertpress.com

ISBN-13: 978-1-95152-748-8 (paperback)
ISBN-13: 978-1-95152-749-5 (e-book)

Business Expert Press Business Law and Corporate Risk Management Collection

Collection ISSN: 2333-6722 (print)
Collection ISSN: 2333-6730 (electronic)

Cover and interior design by Exeter Premedia Services Private Ltd., Chennai, India

First edition: 2020

10 9 8 7 6 5 4 3 2 1

Printed in the United States of America.

Abstract

Various risks, security issues, and disasters have occurred environmentally and in the corporate world (Peters 2018; Gheuens et al. 2019). Mitigation can be used for risks and security occurrences if using an appropriate approach. There must be a specific approach to mitigate the situation and further recommend mitigation strategies. Experts are required to identify the associated risks and securities early enough to safeguard the situation and minimize the impact. Risk and security management plays a major role in situations of uncertainty. The following are some relevant questions to risk and security management: How can this situation be forecasted and taken care of early in similar situations? Can these occurrences be captured historically? Can such patterns of occurrences be identified? Can the data relating to the occurrences be captured? Can the data be used to predict future occurrences? Can the relevance of the data be an important factor? Is security important? What happens if the data are manipulated? How are the data manipulated? How can the data be protected and secured? Security is the driving factor in risk management and plays an important role in the data.

Various types of risk and security apply to various industries, business functions, roles, and responsibilities. This book intends to illustrate top business cases and use cases that apply to respective industries by suggesting ways to define, analyze, monitor, control, and mitigate risk (Morosan and DeFranco 2019; Aydos et al. 2019). This approach mitigates risk using data and by putting corrective action in place. Such analysis takes time because humans cannot quickly analyze huge amounts of data. People can use data science, data analytics, and machine learning (ML) algorithms to speed the process.

Artificial intelligence (AI) enables machines to learn from previous human experiences through continuous learning from new sets of input data. The development of mathematical algorithms has led to the marked creation of ML and to the AI revolution today.

In this book, AI will be used to mitigate risks through various case studies that the reader will understand and benefit from. AI produces effective and dramatic results in business. Many organizations desire to understand and improve risk management skills to improve their chances of handling risk.

Risk and security has become important everywhere because of the large volume of data, different velocity, and variety of data. These aspects of life appear to be growing larger and more frequent and are often accompanied by negative impacts. People can use an undetermined amount of risk to strengthen their position. The range and breadth of risk and security creates havoc everywhere in the world, and on a variety of projects. Risk and security management is important in an organization because without it, the organization may have trouble defining its objectives. The most important reason for strategy implementation is fear of financial loss. This book focuses on problem statements with appropriate use cases and proposes AI solutions using data science and ML approaches.

In this book, we hope to provide concrete answers to the crucial questions facing so many organizations: Where are these risks and security issues and what can be done to lower their impacts? Is AI part of the answers to the risk and security mitigations?

Keywords

project management; construction management; program management; skills development; risk, security; artificial intelligence; analytics; machine learning; mitigation; performance review; data science, and business intelligence

Contents

Acknowledgments

Our experts on artificial intelligence (AI) designs and solutions for risk and security have worked across the corporate world to acquire knowledge and expertise. AI and risk researchers have had a profound impact on our thinking and on the contents of this book. Subsequently, serving many corporate customers has greatly influenced the preparation of this material.

Thank you to our parents, Godson Addo, Mary (Vanderpuije) Addo, Seetharaman Centhala, Thulasi Centhala, K. Shanmugam, and S. Saroja, for encouraging us to get an education and work diligently in our field of work. We do not think we would have made it this far without their support.

We would like to extend gratitude to our families: Louvaine Addo, Mala Srini, and Kavitha Muthu; Archie's and Srini's children: Koushik Seethula, Shashank Seethula, and Srima Seethula; and Muthu's children: Maanasa Muthu and Sarvesh Muthu for their collective patience with our busy schedules.

Thank you to Editide for copyediting. We would like to extend gratitude to Venkat and everyone at Bizstats Technologies Pvt. Ltd. who enabled us to be a Software-as-a-Service BizStats.AI company, which provided major input to write this book.

CHAPTER 1

Introduction

- Target audience
- What do you get from the book?
- What this book covers?
- This book's mind map
- Organization of chapters
  - o Artificial intelligence (AI) project architecture and design
  - o Introduction to risk
  - o Introduction to security
  - o Introduction to the AI knowledge base
  - o How AI, risk, and security come together
  - o Business use cases
  - o AI solutions for risk
  - o AI solutions for security
  - o Industry domain
  - o Functional domain
  - o Futuristic AI
- Conclusion
- References

Chapter Outline

- Book introduction
- Organization of the book
- Chapter introduction

Key Learning Points

- Learn and understand introduction

Target Audience

This book mainly focuses on how AI can be applied to risk and security management. This book follows current trends of AI in the branch of natural language processing, natural language question and answering systems of AI, conversational AI in risk and security domains, AI supporting drones, AI Cybersecurity, Internet of Things devices, and use cases.

Applicable AI topics are targeted toward:

- Corporate top executives, founders, chief technology officers, chief information officers, chief data officers, chief security officers, chief risk officers, data scientists, data architects, AI designers, AI engineers, project managers, and consultants to understand how to manage risk and security using AI.
- Students, teachers, and developers will find this book useful and practical. It will provide an overview of many AI components and introduce how AI can be used in large, medium, and small corporate environments.
- Anybody who strives to understand how AI can be used for risk and security.

What Do You Get From the Book?

- Understand and learn how to apply AI to risk and security.
- Design and apply knowledge-based AI solutions to solve risk and security problems.
- Architecture and design of AI systems relies on the following:
  o Subject matter experts: This means having a practical view of how solutions can be used, not just developed. Case studies of risk and security are used as examples in the book.
  o Appropriately applied mathematics and algorithms are used in this book. Do not skip the mathematical equations if you have the need to study them. AI relies heavily on mathematics.
  o Applied physics and usage into hardware systems and futuristic approaches from quantum computers to parallel

processing of network of quantum computer handlings. AI is still evolving. Give your full attention to new concepts and applied creative ideas in the futuristic AI chapter.

o Decision theory, decision-making process, and the Markov decision process algorithm (Gupta and Katarya 2018).

What This Book Covers

This book introduces how AI is applied to corporations; start-ups; and large, medium, and small companies to help automate the tedious jobs of maintaining risk and security. Automation helps the working environment of the organizations by applying AI and machine learning to aid human experts.

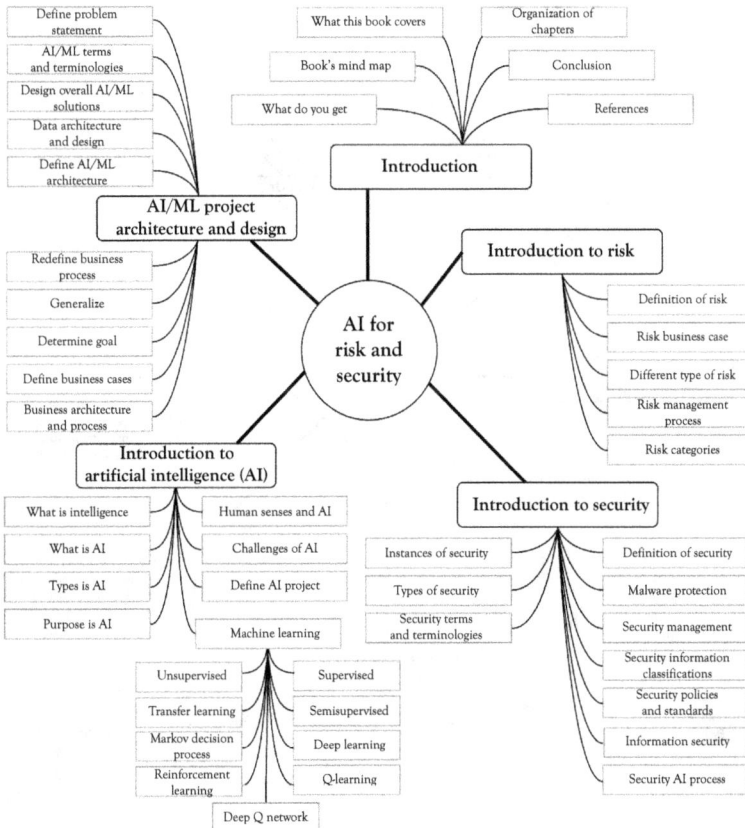

Figure 1.1 Mind map of the book

- How does a company get true value from AI?
- What are the business use cases for AI with visionary?
- How do I identify the best business case for AI adoption and evaluate opportunities?
- Should I build or buy an AI platform?
- How do I find and recruit top AI talent for my enterprise?
- How will I bring AI into my business to increase revenue or decrease costs?
- How can I facilitate AI adoption within my organization?

Dealing with data includes data collection, data preparation, data transformation, securing the data, using the data to align with an organization's AI use case, and much more.

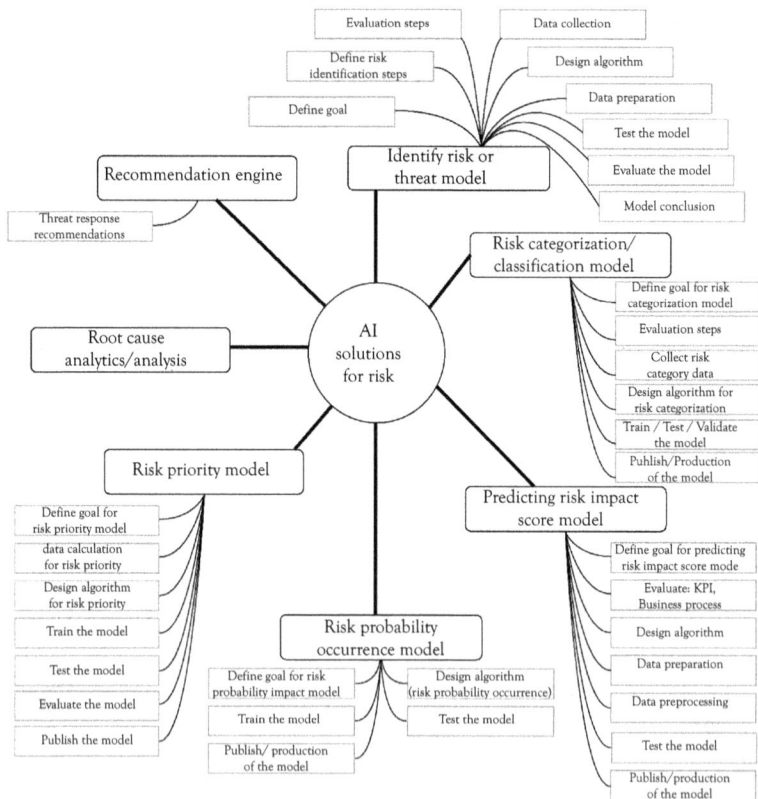

Figure 1.2 Mind map of AI solution for risk

A mind map for the book introduction is provided in Figure 1.1. This gives the reader a direction of what is covered in the book and organization of chapters.

See Figure 1.2. This gives the reader a direction of what risk areas are covered with AI solutions in the book.

See Figure 1.3. This gives the reader a direction of what security areas are covered with AI solutions in the book.

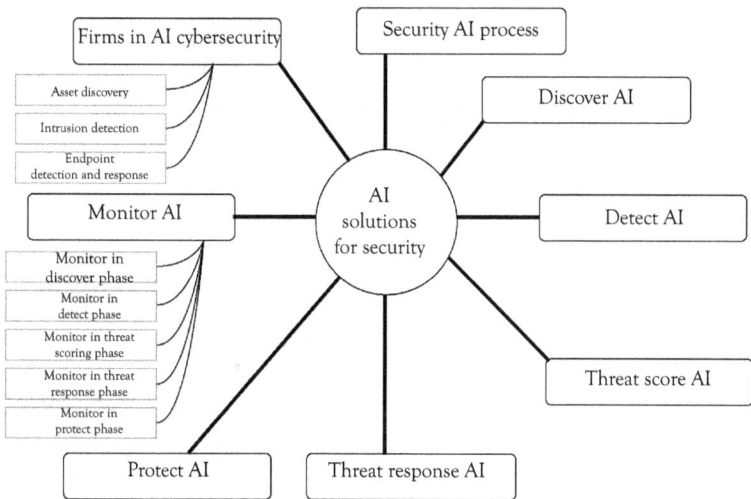

Figure 1.3 Mind map of AI solutions for security

CHAPTER 2

Artificial Intelligence/ Machine Learning Project Architecture and Design

- Introduction to artificial intelligence (AI) and machine learning (ML) project architecture and design
- Illustrated steps to start an AI and ML project architecture and design perspective
- How to build and design specifically for ML and AI use cases

Chapter Outline

- Architecture and design perspective of AI and ML projects
- Comparison of current architecture and future architecture
- Data analytics and life cycle
- Data processing steps
- Future cleaning and extraction
- ML algorithms

Key Learning Points

- Learn and understand how AI and ML project architecture and design is carried over

AI and ML Project Architecture and Design Steps

- Define the problem statement
- Understand existing and current business architectures and business processes
- Define business cases and use cases
- Determine goal
- AI and ML apply to business architectures and business processes
  - o Generalize the problem, use case, and business process
  - o Redefine the overall process
  - o Translate into AI and ML problem statements
- Define AI and ML architecture

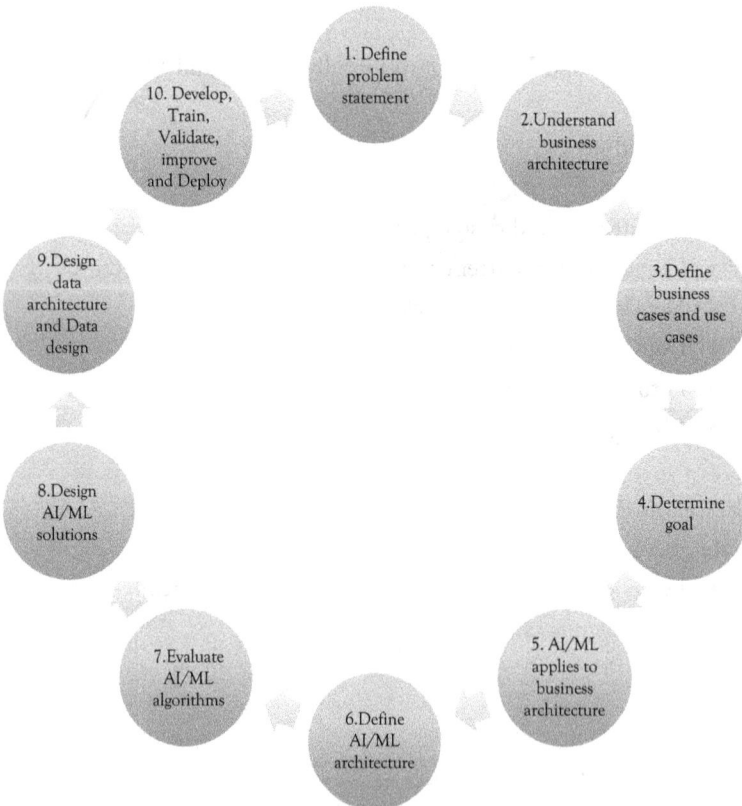

Figure 2.1 AI and ML project architecture and design process

- Evaluate the available AI and ML algorithms to decide the architecture
- Design the overall AI and ML solutions
- Design data architecture and data design
- Develop, train, validate, improve, and deploy

See Figure 2.1 AI and ML project architecture and design process for the detail architecture and design steps.

Terms and Terminologies

An **actor** in the Unified Modeling Language is a role played by a user (stakeholder) or any other system that interacts with the subject. The actor interacts with the subject, for example, an organization data and the resources manipulating the data. Another example is the primary actor of a use case is the stakeholder that calls on the system to deliver one of its services.

Define Problem Statement

A problem statement is a description of an issue to be addressed or a condition to be improved upon based on the requirement in question (Jain et al. 2018). Usually, there is a gap between the current problem statement and desired goal statement of a process or product.

Look at the five W's (who, what, when, where, and why) to define the problem statement clearly with past, present, and future states.

- Who: define the actors to the problem or system and the process involved.
- What: define the problems and the objectives of the problem.
- When: define time during the occurrence of specific event or action.
- Where: define where it happened or where it is expected to happen.
- Why: define why this is happening, why it happened, or why it will happen.

Add "how" into this mix to understand the problem clearly. Look at the big picture and analyze previous issues, current issues, and future issues. Define the desired state of how problems will be solved.

Examples of Problem Statements

ML and AI for Risk

Risks are involved in every action. It is a continuous problem to manually monitor the risks and mitigate large tasks (Rona-Tas et al., 2019). Solve this problem using ML and AI approaches.

ML and AI for Security

Security is a big problem for corporate and government organizations (McGraw et al., 2019). This problem can be solved using ML and AI approaches.

Problem statements are defined very generically and may not focus on the correct problem statements. These statements can be divided into multiple problem statements; this process is illustrated in the AI solutions for risk and AI solutions for security chapters.

Understand Existing and Current Business Architectures and Business Processes

Ask the following questions when examining old and new business architectures:

- Who are the stakeholders, customers, users, and organizations?
- How should you define your vision, strategies, tactics, policies, rules, and regulations?
- What is the value stream through initiatives and projects and how is it measured?
- What capabilities are enabled and what proposals are made using gathered information?

See Figure 2.2.

Business Architecture

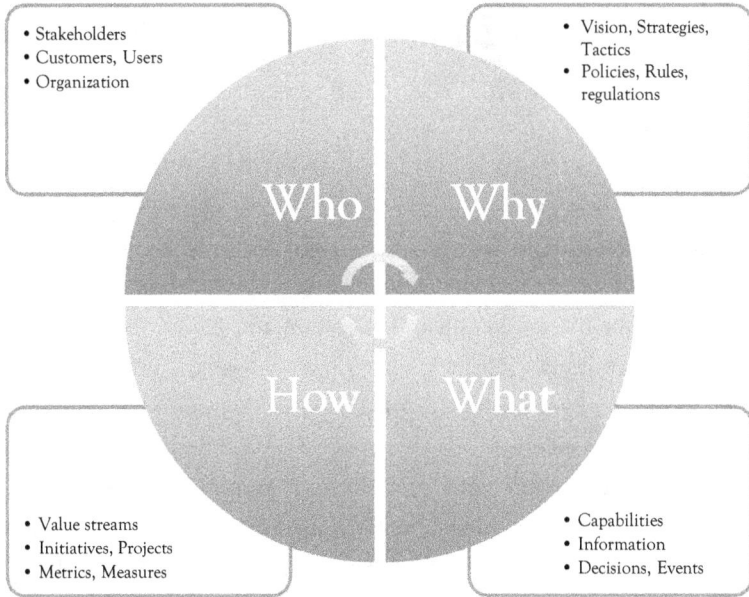

• Stakeholders
• Customers, Users
• Organization

• Vision, Strategies, Tactics
• Policies, Rules, regulations

Who   Why

How   What

• Value streams
• Initiatives, Projects
• Metrics, Measures

• Capabilities
• Information
• Decisions, Events

Figure 2.2 Business architecture process

Business Process

Business architecture is further broken down into the business process (Vaez-Alaei et al. 2018). The business process defines how the business operates, manages, and serves to meet the businesses' objectives. Each organization may have unique business processes in the industry and functional areas. See Figure 2.3.

Typically, chief executive officers are responsible for strategies, infrastructures, products, and services. Chief marketing officers are

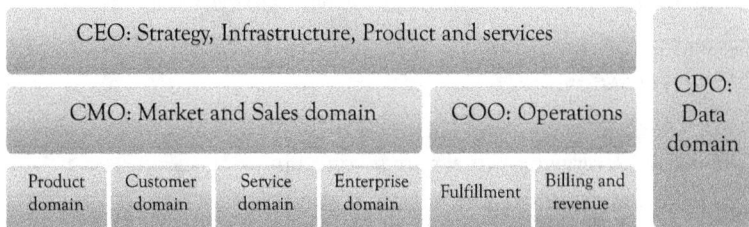

CEO: Strategy, Infrastructure, Product and services

CMO: Market and Sales domain

COO: Operations

CDO: Data domain

Product domain

Customer domain

Service domain

Enterprise domain

Fulfillment

Billing and revenue

Figure 2.3 Typical business process

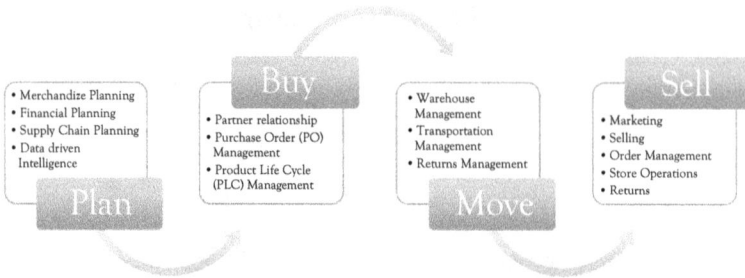

Figure 2.4 Retail industry typical business processes

responsible for the marketing and sales domain. Chief operating offi-cers are responsible for business operations. Nowadays, most organiza-tions have introduced a new top management position called a chief data officer who manages data architecture, data design, data collec-tion, data management, data processing, applying data science, ML, and AI. This role helps industries keep up with the latest technology transformations, such as moving to the Cloud infrastructure, ML, AI, and Internet of Things. In fact, all existing business processes are in the process of re-engineering and redefining to adopt technological trans-formations, including risk and security. All business functional areas and related business processes are at risk. This book illustrates how to automate business functional areas and related business processes using ML and AI.

Look at the retail industry business process at a very high level. See Figure 2.4.

Define Business Cases

The business case must be defined for the problem statement (Haas et al. 2019). This process is illustrated for ML and AI using risk problem statements.

Problem Statements:

- Risk is everywhere. Risks are involved in every action. It is a continuous problem to manually monitor risks and mitigate, especially in the case of huge tasks. The goal is to solve this huge problem by using ML and AI approaches.

- Security is a very big problem for corporate and government organizations and could be solved using ML and AI approaches.

Identify Return on Investment (ROI) and Benefits:
Organizations will save money on a daily basis by implementing ML and AI systems for risk and security. The human workforce will be free from manually identifying and mitigating risks and security. Approximate estimation of ROI would be at least $10,000, but this number depends on the size of the organization and the current time spent on the manual risk and security tasks. ML and AI also eliminate 24/7 watchdog risk and security tasks.

Strategic Alignment:
Strategic alignment should align with business goals. The business goal of all organizations is to use the data to drive decisions and automation. The ML and AI implementation for risk and security aligns with the business goals.

Investment: The investment would be minimal as it will be Software as a Service in the Cloud.

Values:
The organization will have peace of mind. The customers and partnering organizations will have more confidence.

Efficiency:
The organization's operational processes and automation will be improved by 60 times.

Define Use Cases

In this step, define or identify the use cases to be supported to a tangible outcome (Refactoring to Improve the Security Quality of Use Case Models 2019). Most of the ML and AI projects are diverted into research and development (R&D) projects, the reason being that use cases are identified up front. Use cases vary by industry and by business function, but some of them are listed below.

Financial and banking industry:

- Prevention of credit loss and fraud.

- Avoidance of money laundering.
- Compliance with industry standards and government clauses.

Retail industry:

- Avoidance of data breaches.
- Improve market share by competitive pricing.

Determine the Goal

The goal of ML and AI risk solutions is to capture all the risks items to identify, classify, and prioritize risks and gain prevention recommendations.

The goal of the ML and AI security solutions is to prevent threats in real time. ML and AI security systems discover, detect, provide threat scores, threat protection, and prevention recommendations.

Before going through each of the ML and AI project architecture and design steps, let us look at the typical data analytics project and its life cycle. Multiple streams of data analytics and life cycle projects may be needed to define the overall project architecture and design.

Data Analytics and Life Cycle

The data analytics life cycle is designed for large data problems and data science projects (Sahoo and Mohanty 2018). There are six phases, and the project work can occur in several phases simultaneously. The cycle is iterative to portray a real project. The work can return to previous phases as new information is uncovered. The data analytics life cycle consists of the following sequence of steps:

Data analytics life cycle overview:

1. Phase 1: Discovery
2. Phase 2: Data preparation
3. Phase 3: Model planning
4. Phase 4: Model building
5. Phase 5: Communicate results
6. Phase 6: Operationalize

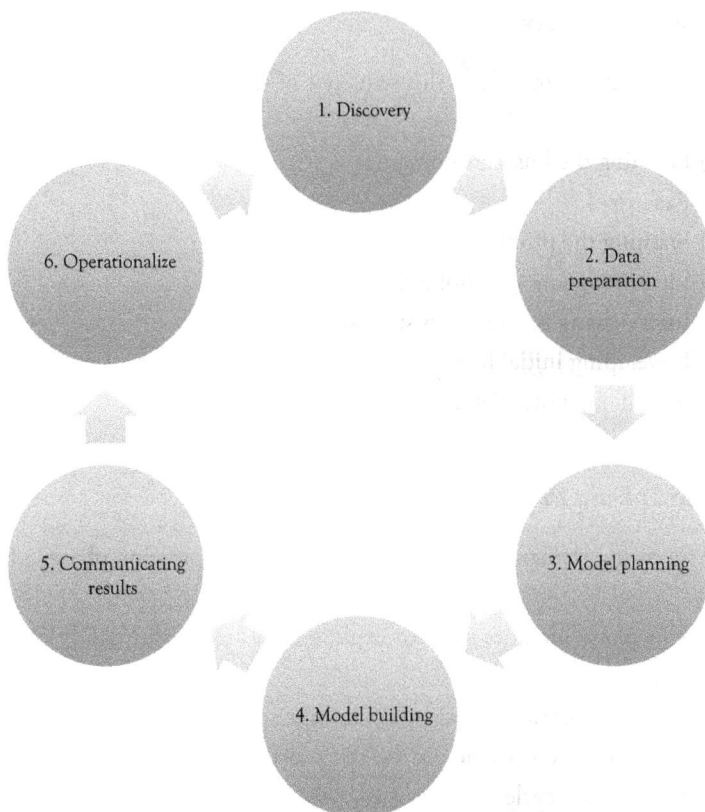

Figure 2.5 Data analytics life cycle

The data scientist is the main analytics stakeholder. The data scientist provides analytic techniques and modeling. The other members are the team are as follows:

1. Business user: understands the domain area.
2. Project sponsor: provides high-level requirements and budgeting.
3. Project manager/agile/scrum master: ensures that objectives are met.
4. Data architect: provides business domain expertise based on deep understanding of the data.
5. Data engineer: provides technical skills, assists with data management and extraction, and supports analytic development areas.

Here are the steps that go into the process. See Figure 2.5.

Phase 1: Discovery

The discovery phase follows this sequence of steps:

- (a) Learning the business domain
- (b) Resources
- (c) Framing the problem
- (d) Identifying key stakeholders
- (e) Interviewing the analytics sponsor
- (f) Developing initial hypotheses
- (g) Identifying potential data sources

Phase 2: Data Preparation

The following elements are included in the data preparation phase:

- (a) This phase includes steps to explore, preprocess, and condition the data.
- (b) This phase creates a healthy environment and analytics sandbox.
- (c) Data preparation tends to be the most labor-intensive step in the analytics life cycle.
- (d) At least 50 percent of the time for the tasks is spent in the data preparation phase.
- (e) The data preparation phase is generally the most iterative and the phase that teams tend to underestimate.

The data preparation stage requires development workspaces. Preparation of the workplace is beneficial for the following reasons:

- It creates an analytic workspace.
- It allows the team to explore data without interfering with live production data.
- A prepared workspace collects a variety of data (expansive approach).
- The workspace allows organizations to undertake ambitious projects beyond traditional data analysis.

- This concept is acceptable to data science teams and IT groups.

In the workspace, the extract, transform, load, and transform functions may be performed based on the team (System and Method for Providing Predictive Behavioral Analytics 2018):

The extract, transform, and load users may perform extract, transform, and load functions.

In the workspace, the extract, load, and transform process preserves raw data, which can be useful for examination.

Example: In a financial organizations' credit card fraud detection, high-risk transactions may be carelessly filtered out or transformed before being loaded into the database.

Learning about the data is important for the following reasons:

(a) It determines the data available to the team early in the project.
(b) It highlights gaps and identifies data not currently available.
(c) It identifies data outside the organization that might be useful.

Data Conditioning

The data should be conditioned for several reasons, such as cleaning data, normalizing datasets, and performing transformations. This task is viewed as the step prior to data analysis, and the step might be performed by the data owner, IT department, and database administrator. Data scientists should be involved. It is a known fact that data science teams prefer too much data rather than too little.

Here are questions and observations that must be addressed when analyzing the data, along with the chapters where you can find further information on these topics.

Chapter 3: What are the data sources and target fields?
Chapter 4: How clean is the data?
Chapter 5: How consistent are the contents and files? Are there missing or inconsistent values?
Chapter 6: Assess the consistency of the data types (numeric, alphanumeric)?

Chapter 7: Review the contents to ensure the data makes sense.

Chapter 8: Look for evidence of systematic error.

Survey and Visualize

Specific data visualization tools may be used to gain an overview of the data (Wang et al. 2019). This process starts with overview and on-demand zoom and filter details. This approach enables the user to find areas of interest and zoom and filter to find more detailed data.

The following questions and observations must be addressed when surveying and visualizing data.

Chapter 1: Review data to ensure calculations are consistent.

Chapter 2: Does the data distribution stay consistent?

Chapter 3: Assess the details of the data, the range of values, and the level of aggregation of the data.

Chapter 4: Does the data represent the population of interest?

Chapter 5: Check time-related variables: daily, weekly, monthly? Are these variables sufficient?

Chapter 6: Is the data standardized or normalized? Are the data scales consistent?

Chapter 7: In the case of geospatial datasets, are state and country abbreviations consistent?

Tools for data preparation are Hadoop, Alpine Miner, OpenRefine, Data Wrangler, and Google Cloud data preparation.

- Hadoop can perform parallel consume and analysis.
- Alpine Miner provides a graphical user interface for creating analytic workflows.
- OpenRefine (formerly Google Refine) is a free, open-source tool to use with messy data.
- Data Wrangler is an interactive tool for data cleansing and transformation.
- Google Cloud provides data preparation.

Phase 3: Data Modeling

In this phase, the following steps are conducted:

- Determine the structure of the data to help determine the tools and analytic techniques for the next phase (Palli et al. 2019).
- Determine the analytic techniques that will enable the team to meet business objectives and accept or reject the working hypotheses.
- Decide on a single model or a series of techniques as part of a larger analytic workflow.
- Understand how similar problems have been analyzed in the past.

Phase 4: Model Building

The following tasks are considered in model building:

1. Execute the models defined in Phase 3.
2. Develop datasets for training, testing, and production.
3. Develop models on training data and test-on-test data.
4. Questions to consider:

(a) Does the model appear valid and accurate on the test data?
(b) Does the model output and behavior make sense to the domain experts?
(c) Do the parameter values make sense in the context of the domain?
(d) Will the model sufficiently and accurately meet the goal?
(e) Can the model avoid intolerable mistakes?
(f) Are more data or inputs needed?
(g) Will the type of model chosen support the run-time environment?
(h) Will a different model be required to address the business problem?

Common model building tools are: R and PL/R—PL/R, Python, SQL, Octave, WEKA, SAS, SPSS Modeler, MATLAB, Alpine Miner, STATISTICA, and MATHEMATICA.

Phase 5: Communication Results

The following steps should be followed when communicating results:

1. Determine if the team succeeded or failed in its objectives.
2. Determine if the results are statistically significant and valid.
3. If the results are significant and valid, identify aspects of the results that present relevant findings.
4. Determine if the results are in line with the hypotheses.
5. Communicate the results and major insights derived from the analysis.

Phase 6: Operationalize

The following occurs in the operationalize phase:

1. The team communicates the benefits of the project.
2. The team sets up a pilot project to deploy the work in a controlled way.
3. Risks are managed and corrective action is taken by undertaking small scope and pilot deployment before a wide-scale rollout.
4. During the pilot project:

(a) The team may execute the algorithm more efficiently in the database rather than with in-memory tools like R, especially with larger datasets.
(b) To test the model in a live setting, consider running the model in a production environment for a discrete set of products or a single line of business.
(c) Monitor model accuracy and retrain the model if necessary.

Let us look at the ML algorithms mind map and define the terms and terminologies used in the mind map.

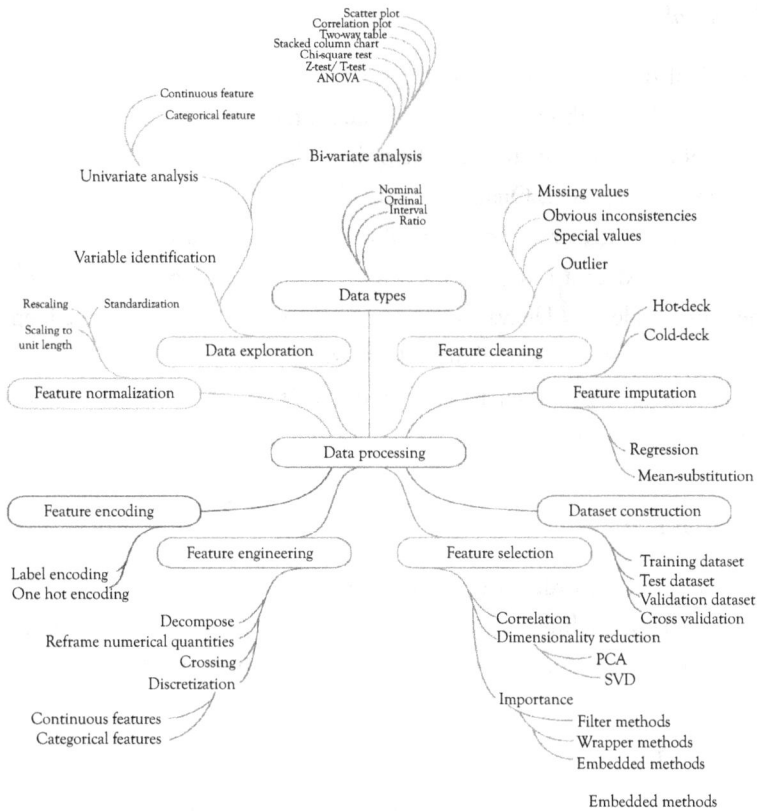

Figure 2.6 ML and AI data processing map

ML Data Processing

Data processing is important in any analytical project, data project, or ML and AI project. Most of the time is spent in this step (Kotenko et al. 2019).

See Figure 2.6.

Some of the statistics-related items are discussed here. If you want to know more about the terms and terminologies, please reference a statistics book. Figure 2.6 explains the required steps needed to process data and lists statistical experiments and measuring methods.

The first step in the data processing is to determine the statistical data type or levels of measurement by examining different techniques (Overgoor et al. 2019; Ohanian 2019).

Nominal Data

Nominal data (also known as nominal scale) is a type of data used to label variables without providing any quantitative value. It is the simplest form of a scale of measure. Unlike ordinal data, nominal data cannot be ordered or measured. Qualitative classifications include variables such as city, name, state, or any categorical data, which has a numerical representation tied to a categorical attribute value. For example, the gender field in a table (0 = Unavailable, 1 = Male, and 2 = Female). These identifiers represent actual attribute values. Nominal data type should not be applied with any mathematical operations. The order is not a valid. The central tendency for nominal data type is mode.

Ordinal Data

Ordinal data are orderable or can be ranked; for example: 0 = low, 2 = high, and 1 = medium. With ordinal data, the ordering is very important and central tendency to ordinal data is mode or median.

Interval Data

The items should also be measured to quantify and compare differences between them. For example, temperature as measured in Fahrenheit or Celsius.

Interval scales are numeric scales where both the order and the exact differences are valid. For example, the difference between 60 and 50 degrees is a measurable 10 degrees, as is the difference between 80 and 70 degrees. The central tendency can be measured by mode and median, and standard deviation can also be calculated.

Ratio Data

Ratio data are any numeric data that is measurable, orderable, can be ranked, and can be applied to any mathematical calculation. For example: height, weight, duration, sales amount, and profit amount. The central tendency for the ratio data is mode, mean, median, average, and orderable. See Table 2.1.

Table 2.1 Ratio data

Provides	Nominal	Ordinal	Interval	Ratio
Order of value	No	Yes	Yes	Yes
Frequency distribution (count)	Yes	Yes	Yes	Yes
Mode	Yes	Yes	Yes	Yes
Median	No	Yes	Yes	Yes
Mean	No	No	Yes	Yes
Quantify the difference	No	No	Yes	Yes

Data Exploration

Data exploration analyzes data using visual exploration to understand the dataset and determine data characteristics such as size, amount of data, completeness of the data, correctness of the data, and the relationship between data elements (Alvarez-Ayllon 2018).

Variable Identification

Variable identification is the basis for any input (predicator) or output (target) to ML models. Variable identification determines what kind of variables can be used as a predicator or target.

Univariate Analysis

Univariate analysis is a statistical analysis that determines the variable or multiple variables involved. This analysis applies to categorical variables and features (qualitative) or numerical (quantitative) univariate data. Categorical univariate data consist of numbers such as height or weight.

Typically, univariate is visualized using a frequency distribution table, bar chart, histograms, frequency polygons, and pie charts.

1. Continuous features
2. Categorical features

Bivariate Analysis

Bivariate analysis is the statistical analysis of two variables (attributes) and explores the relationship between two variables. Bivariate analysis determines the strength of the association between variables. This analysis examines the differences between two variables and the significance of the differences.

Types of bivariate analysis include numerical versus numerical, categorical versus categorical, and numerical versus categorical. Bivariate analysis is illustrated through any one of the following visualizations.

Scatter Plot

A scatter plot explores two numerical values to provide a visual representation of the linear and nonlinear relationships.

Linear correlation quantifies the strength of a linear relationship using the following formula.

$$Cov(X,Y) = \frac{\sum (x - \bar{x})(y - \bar{y})}{n}$$

where x(dash) and y(dash) are the sample mean, and n is the number of samples.

Correlation Plot

Correlation plots are used to assess whether or not correlations are consistent across groups.

1. Two-way table
2. Stacked column chart

Chi-Square Test

Chi-square test is a statistical hypothesis test where the sampling distribution of the test statistic is a chi-squared distribution when the NULL hypothesis is true. The Pearson's chi-square test is commonly used. The chi-square test is used to determine if a significant difference exists between the expected frequencies and the observed frequencies in one or more categories. The chi-square test gives P value.

Chi-square formula:

$$x^2 = Sigma \frac{(Observed - Expected)^2}{Expected}$$

Z-Test/T-Test

The Z-test and T-test are the same. It is a statistical evaluations of the averages of two groups and determines the differences and significance of the differences.

$$Z = \frac{\bar{X}_1 - \bar{X}_2}{\sqrt{\left(\frac{S_1^2}{N_1} + \frac{S_2^2}{N_2}\right)}}$$

Where :

$\bar{X}_1, \bar{X}_2$: *Averages*

S_1^2, S_2^2 : *Variances*

N_1, N_2 : *Counts*

Z : *Standard Normal Distribution*

$$t = \frac{\bar{X}_1 - \bar{X}_2}{\sqrt{S^2\left(\frac{1}{N_1} + \frac{1}{N_2}\right)}}$$

$$S^2 = \frac{(N_1 - 1)S_1^2 + (N_2 - 1)S_2^2}{N_1 + N_2 - 2}$$

Where

$\bar{X}_1, \bar{X}_2$: *Averages*

S_1^2, S_2^2 : *Variances*

N_1, N_2 : *Counts*

t : has t distribution with $N_1 + N_2 - 2$ degree of freedom

Analysis of Variance (ANOVA)

The ANOVA is a short form variance test that statistically measures the averages of more than two groups that are statistically different from each other. In simple terms, the test determines the statistically significant differences between the mean values of three or more independent groups.

Feature Cleaning

Feature cleaning is another name for data cleaning. Clean and quality data determine the success of a data project. Collecting quality data is the biggest challenge.

Missing values

Null values, spaces, or no value can be present in the data.

Obvious Inconsistencies

Inconsistent data problems arise when various information systems are collecting, processing, and updating data due to human or equipment reasons.

Inconsistent data make it impossible to obtain correct information from the data and reduce data availability.

Special Values

The special values are specific to the respective dataset. For example, some default values for a date field are represented as "1900-01-01" for effective begin date and "2099-12-31" for effective end date.

Outlier

In statistics, an outlier is a data point that differs significantly from other observations (Huang et al., 2019). An outlier can cause serious problems in statistical analysis and feature cleaning.

Feature Imputation:

- Hot deck
- Cold deck

- Mean substitution
- Regression

Feature Engineering:

- Decompose
- Discretization
- Continuous features
- Categorical features
- Reframe numerical quantities
- Crossing

Feature Selection:

- Correlation
- Dimensionality reduction
- Principal component analysis (PCA)
- Singular value decomposition (SVD)
- Importance
- Filter methods
- Wrapper methods
- Embedded methods

Feature Encoding:
- Label encoding
- One hot encoding

Feature Normalization:

- Rescaling
- Standardization
- Scaling to unit length

Dataset Construction:

- Training dataset
- Test dataset
- Validation dataset
- Cross-validation

ML Algorithm Mind Map

See Figure 2.7.

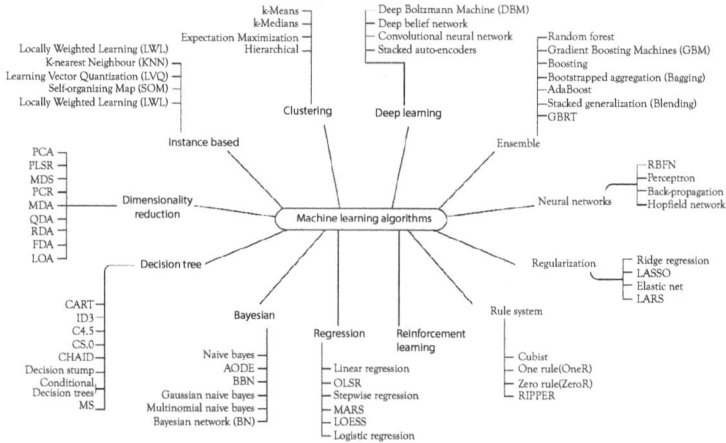

Figure 2.7 ML algorithm mind map

ML Algorithms

A ML algorithm is a method used to process data to extract patterns that can be applied in a new situation (Andriosopoulos et al. 2019). The goal is to apply a system to a specific input–output transformation task.

ML and deep learning are embraced by ML algorithms. ML is a class of methods for automatically creating models from data. ML algorithms turn a dataset into a model, which is effective with supervised, unsupervised, classification, and regression algorithms.

Typical examples are real-valued labels, which are the amount of rainfall or the height of a person. The first five algorithms are linear regression, logistic regression, classification and regression trees, Naïve Bayes, and *k-nearest neighbors* algorithm. These algorithms are examples of supervised learning.

Classification

Gmail is an e-mail application by Google that uses ML techniques to determine if an e-mail received is a spam based on the sender, recipients, subject, and message body of the e-mail. Classification takes a set of data with known labels and labels new records based on that information.

Further classification is a family of supervised ML algorithms that designate input as belonging to a predefined class.

Some common use cases for classification include:

1. Credit card fraud detection.
2. E-mail spam detection.
3. Classification data are labeled, for example: spam and nonspam or fraud and nonfraud. ML assigns new data to a class.
4. Classification based on predetermined features.
5. Features the "if" questions.
6. The label answers the "if" questions, for example: if it walks, flies, and whistles like a bird, the label is "bird."

Clustering

Clustering can be used for search results grouping, grouping of customers, anomaly detection, and text categorization.

Google News uses a technique called clustering to group news articles into categories based on title and content. Clustering algorithms discover groupings that occur in collection of data. Clustering places objects into categories by analyzing similarities between inputs.

Clustering uses unsupervised ML algorithms that do not have the outputs in advance:

1. Clustering uses the K-means algorithm to initialize all the coordinates to centroids.
2. With every pass of the algorithm, each point is assigned to its nearest centroid based on some distance metric, usually Euclidean distance.
3. The centroids are updated to be the "centers" of all the points assigned to it in that pass.
4. This process repeats until a minimum change in the centers occurs.

K-means Clustering

The K-means clustering algorithm is popular because it can be applied to relatively large sets of data. The user specifies the number of clusters to be found and the algorithm separates the data into spherical clusters by finding a set of cluster centers, assigning each observation to a cluster, and determining new cluster centers.

The sample space is initially partitioned into K-clusters and the observations are randomly assigned to the clusters. For each sample, the distance from the observation to the centroid of the cluster should be calculated. If the sample is closest to its own cluster, leave it or select another cluster.

Repeat steps 1 and 2 until no observations are moved from one cluster to another. When the clusters are stable, each sample is assigned a cluster, which results in the lowest possible distance to the centroid of the cluster.

Collaborative Filtering

Amazon uses a ML technique called collaborative filtering (commonly referred to as recommendation) to determine which products users will like based on their history and similarity to other users who bought similar products.

Collaborative filtering algorithms recommend items based on preference information from many users. The goal of a collaborative filtering algorithm is (a) to take preferences data from users and (b) to create a model that can be used for recommendations or predictions.

Random Forests

Random forests or random decision forests are a collective learning method for classification, regression, and other tasks. These forests operate by constructing a multitude of decision trees at training time and outputting the mode of the classes (classification) or mean prediction (regression) of the individual trees. Random decision forests compensate for decision trees' habit of overfitting their training set.

Association Rules

The association rules are the statements that show the probability of relationships between data items in large datasets in various types of databases. Association rule mining has several applications and is widely used to help discover sales correlations in transactional data or discover diagnoses in medical data. Other applications use associated rules in decision making.

Regression

Regression is used frequently in finance statistical measurements, investing, and other disciplines that attempt to determine the strength of the relationships between one dependent variable (usually denoted by Y) and a series of other changing variables (known as independent variables) (Liu et al. 2019).

Typical regressions such as linear regression can be used to quantify the relative impacts of age, gender, and diet (the predictor variables) on height (the outcome variable). Linear regression is also known as multiple regression, multivariate regression, ordinary least squares, and regression. Regression techniques are used for predictive modeling and data mining tasks. On average, only two or three types of regression are commonly used.

Linear Regression

Linear regression is a ML algorithm based on supervised learning. Regression models target prediction values based on independent variables. This algorithm is mostly used to examine the relationship between variables and forecasting. Regression models differ based on the relationship between the dependent and independent variables and the number of independent variables being used.

Linear regression predicts the value of a dependent variable (y) based on a given independent variable (x). This regression technique discovers the linear relationship between x-input and y-output.

Linear regression is used in statistical calculations. In simple linear regression, a single independent variable is used to predict the value of a dependent variable. In multiple linear regression, two or more independent variables are used to predict the value of a dependent variable. The difference between the two is the number of independent variables.

Linear regression can be used to model the relationship between two variables by fitting a linear equation to observed data. One variable is an explanatory variable, and the other is a dependent variable. For example, a modeler might want to relate the weights of individuals to their heights using a linear regression model.

Before attempting to fit a linear model to observed data, a modeler should first determine if there is a relationship between the variables of interest. This does not necessarily mean that one variable causes the other (e.g., higher exam passing scores do not cause higher college grades); however, some significant association is present between the two variables. A scatterplot may be used to determine the strength of the relationship between two variables. If there appears to be no association between the proposed explanatory and dependent variables (i.e., if the scatterplot does not indicate an increasing or decreasing trends), fitting a linear regression model to the data will not provide a useful model. This means another approach, such a problem solution, should be used.

A valuable numerical measure of association between two variables is the correlation coefficient, which is a value between -1 and 1, indicating the strength of the association of the observed data for the two variables. Let us demonstrate how it works out. A linear regression line has an equation of the form $Y = a + bX$, where X is the explanatory variable and Y is the dependent variable. The slope of the line is b, and a is the intercept (the value of y when $x = 0$).

Logistic Regression

Logistic regression is named for the function used at the core of the method: the logistic function. The logistic function is also called the sigmoid function. This function was developed by statisticians to describe properties of population growth in ecology. It is an S-shaped curve that can take any real-valued number and map it into a value between 0 and 1, but never exactly at those limits.

Ordinary Least Square Regression (OLSR)

The OLSR is a generalized linear modeling technique. It is used for estimating all unknown parameters involved in a linear regression model. This technique minimizes the sum of the squares of the difference between the observed variables and the explanatory variables. OLSR is one of the simplest methods of linear regression. The goal of OLSR is to closely fit a function with the data. It is carried out by minimizing the sum of squared errors from the data.

Stepwise Regression

Stepwise regression is a method of fitting regression models with predictive variables carried out by an automatic procedure. In each step, a variable is considered for addition or subtraction from the set of explanatory variables based on specified criterion.

Let us examine an example of how the stepwise regression procedure works by considering a dataset that concerns the hardening of the cement. The goal in this example is to learn how the composition of the cement and the heat evolved during the hardening of the cement. Data were measured and recorded for 13 batches of cement:

Response y: Heat evolved in calories during hardening of cement on a per gram basis.

Predictor $x1$: Percent of tricalcium aluminate.

Predictor $x2$: Percent of tricalcium silicate.

Predictor $x3$: Percent of tetracalcium alumino ferrite.

Predictor $x4$: Percent of dicalcium silicate.

Subsequent steps will need to be taken to arrive at the solution.

Multivariate Adaptive Regression Splines

Multivariate adaptive regression splines is a form of regression analysis introduced by Jerome H. Friedman in 1991. It is a nonparametric regression technique and is an extension of linear models that automatically model nonlinearities and interactions between variables.

Time Series Analysis

Time series analysis develops models that best capture or describe an observed time series to understand the underlying causes. This field of study seeks the "why" behind a time series dataset. It is a sequence of well-defined data points measured at consistent time intervals over a period. This method is used to analyze time series data and extract meaningful statistics and characteristics about the data. This method requires one to make assumptions about the form of the data and decompose the time series into constitution components. The quality of a descriptive model is determined by how well the model describes all available data and how the model better informs the problem domain.

Time series analysis consists of analyzing time series data to extract meaningful statistics and other characteristics of the data. It has the capability to forecast the use of a model to predict future values based on previously observed values.

Text Analysis

Text analysis is a method of communication used to describe and interpret the characteristics of a recorded or visual message. The purpose of textual analysis is to describe the content, structure, and functions of the messages embedded in texts.

Prediction

In simple terms, a prediction is a forecast. A prediction can be made with many things, such as a football match or the weather. In the word prediction, "pre" means before and diction is the act of commenting on something. This leads to a guess that may be based on evidence or facts.

Simple steps to determine a prediction are:

1. Collect data using meaningful senses and use senses to make observations.
2. Search for patterns of behavior and or characteristics.
3. Develop statements about what the future observations will be.
4. Test the prediction and observe what happens.

The best way to predict with ML is to approach the problem by hiding the uncertainty related to that prediction.

Prediction intervals provide a way to quantify and communicate the uncertainty in a prediction. Confidence intervals can be used to quantify the uncertainty in the dataset population. The mean and standard deviation can be used as parameters for each of the prediction items in question.

A prediction interval can be estimated analytically for simple models, but are more challenging for nonlinear ML models.

Anomaly Detection

Anatomy detection identifies unusual items, events, or observations that may be suspicious in a dataset; typically, the anomalies tend to be a problem. Anomalies can create security issues in an organization. Network issues have been associated with bursts of activities. The patterns do not add up to the common statistical definition of an outlier. This may create failure in unsupervised methods but can be aggregated appropriately to obtain expected results. The cluster analysis algorithm may be used to detect the microcluster pattern successfully. Anomaly techniques are broken into three categories: unsupervised anomaly detection, supervised anomaly detection, and semi-supervised anomaly detection.

Deep Learning

Deep learning is sometimes referred to as structured learning or hierarchical learning. Deep learning is part of ML methods based on artificial

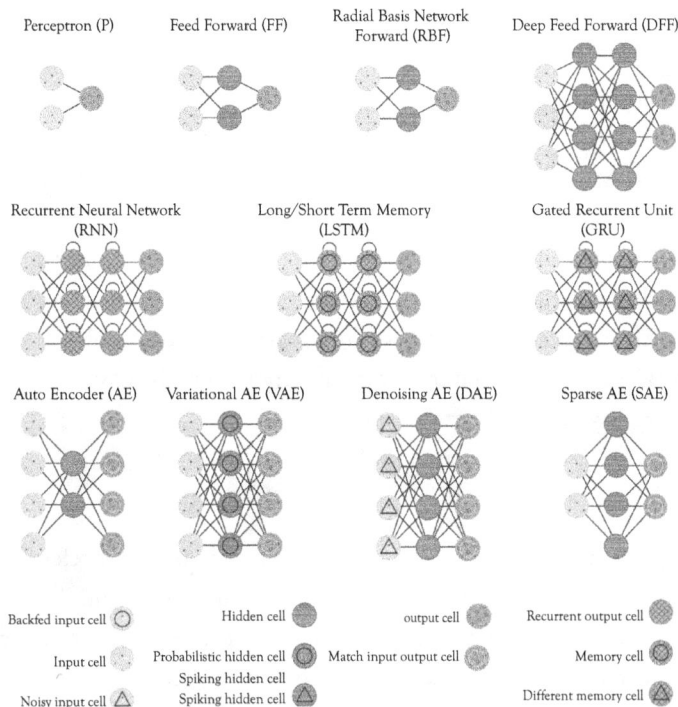

Figure 2.8 Neural network types

neural networks. The learning can be supervised, semi-supervised, or unsupervised.

Neural Network Types

There different neural networks are shown in Figure 2.8.

Deep Boltzmann Machine (DBM)

The DBM is also called stochastic Hopfield network with hidden units. It is the first neural network capable of learning internal representations and can represent and solve difficult combinatoric problems. It is named after the Boltzmann distribution in statistical mechanics, which is used in their sampling function.

The DBM has the following features:

- An unsupervised, probabilistic, generative model with entirely undirected connections between different layers.
- Contains visible units and multiple layers of hidden units.
- Like result-based management, no intralayer connection exists in DBM; connections only exist between units of the neighboring layers.
- A network of symmetrically connected stochastic binary units.
- DBM can be organized as a bipartite graph with odd layers on one side and even layers on the other.
- Units within the layers are independent of each other but are dependent on neighboring layers.
- Learning is made efficient with layer-by-layer pretraining.
- DBM is fine-tuned by backpropagation after learning the binary features in each layer.

Deep Belief Network

A deep belief network is a generative graphical model and is referred as a class of deep neural networks. The network is composed of multiple layers of latent variables with connections between the layers, but not between units in each layer. If trained on a set without supervision, a deep belief network can learn to probabilistically reconstruct its inputs and act as a feature detector. After this learning step, the network can be further trained with supervision to perform classification.

Convolutional Neural Network

The convolutional neural network is a type of artificial neural network used in image recognition and processing and is specifically designed to process pixel data. A neural network is a system of hardware or software patterned after the operation of neurons in the human brain. A convolutional neural network is a category of neural networks that are very effective in areas such as image recognition and classification.

These networks are used in a variety of areas, including image and pattern recognition, speech recognition, natural language processing (NLP), and video analysis.

Stacked Autoencoders

A stacked autoencoder is a neural network that consists of multiple layers of light autoencoders where the outputs of each layer are wired to the inputs of the successive layer. The stacked autoencoder can be used for classification problems.

Ensemble

An ensemble is a type of supervised learning.

ML examples include medical diagnosis, image processing, prediction, classification, learning association, and regression. The intelligent systems built on ML algorithms have the capability to learn from experience or historical data. A large amount of data is recommended because it provides better insights.

The ensemble is a method used in learning algorithms to construct a set of classifiers and to classify new data points by taking a weighted vote of their predictions. The original ensemble method is Bayesian averaging, but more recent algorithms include error-correcting output coding, bagging, and boosting. Bagging is a way to decrease the variance in the prediction by generating additional data using combinations with repetitions to produce multi-sets of the original data.

Random Forest

Random forest—sometimes referred to as a random decision forest—is a popular ensemble method and can be used to build predictive models for both classification and regression problems. Ensemble methods use multiple learning models to gain better predictive results. Random forest models create an entire forest of random, uncorrelated decision trees to arrive at the best possible answer.

Gradient Boosting Machines

Gradient boosting is one of the most powerful techniques for building predictive models.

The boosting method converts weak learners into strong learners. Each new tree is a fit on a modified version of the original dataset. AdaBoost can be introduced for training purposes, beginning with the AdaBoost Algorithm. The weights are increased for observations after evaluating the first tree. Computation is done to determine classification errors from the second tree. A third tree helps predict the revised residuals. The final ensemble model is created after a specified number of iterations.

Boosting

Boosting is a ML ensemble meta-algorithm for reducing bias and variance in supervised learning. Boosting is a family of ML algorithms that converts weak learners to strong ones.

Bootstrapped Aggregation (Bagging)

The goal of an ensemble model is to bring a group of weak learners together to form a strong learner. Bagging is used when the goal is to reduce the variance of a decision tree. This creates several subsets of data from the sample dataset.

AdaBoost

AdaBoost—also referred to as adaptive boosting—is the first practical boosting algorithm proposed by Freund and Schapire in 1996. AdaBoost focuses on classification problems and aims to convert a set of weak classifiers into a strong one.

Stacked Generalization (Blending)

Stacked generalization is simply a general method of using a high-level model to combine lower level models to achieve greater predictive accuracy. The first step is to collect the output of each model into a new set of data.

Gradient Boosted Regression Trees

Gradient boosting is a ML technique used for regression and classification problems. This technique produces a prediction model in the form of an ensemble of weak prediction models, typically decision trees.

Neural Networks

A neural network is a series of algorithms that recognizes underlying relationships in a set of data using a process that imitates the way the human brain operates. Neural networks can adapt to changing input. The network generates the best possible result without needing to redesign the output criteria.

Radial Basis Function Network

A radial basis function network is a mathematical modeling, radial basis function network that uses radial basis functions as activation functions. The network's output is a linear combination of radial basis functions of the inputs and neuron parameters.

Perceptron

Perceptron is a ML algorithm that provides classified outcomes for computing. It dates back to the 1950s and represents a fundamental example of how ML algorithms develop data.

Backpropagation

Backpropagation requires the derivatives of activation functions to be known at network design time. Backpropagation is commonly used by the gradient descent optimization algorithm to adjust the weight of neurons by calculating the gradient of the loss function.

Hopfield Network

The Hopfield network is a recurrent artificial neural network popularized by John Hopfield in 1982 but described earlier by Little in 1974. The Hopfield nets serve as content-addressable ("associative") memory systems with binary threshold nodes.

Regularization

Regularization is a form of regression that constrains, regularizes, or shrinks the coefficient estimates toward zero. This technique discourages learning a more complex or flexible model to avoid the risk of overfitting. Regularization illustrates that models that overfit the data are complex models that often have too many parameters.

Ridge Regression

Ridge regression is a technique for analyzing multiple regression data that suffer from multicollinearity. When multicollinearity occurs, least squares estimates are unbiased but their variances are large. Multicollinearity (also known as collinearity) is a one-predictor variable in a multiple regression model that can be linearly predicted from others with a substantial degree of accuracy. Multicollinearity generally occurs when there are high correlations between two or more predictor variables. Examples of correlated predictor variables are a person's height and weight, age and sales price of a car, years of education, and annual income.

Least Absolute Shrinkage and Selection Operator (LASSO)

LASSO is a regression analysis method that performs variable selection and regularization to enhance the prediction accuracy and interpretability of the statistical model it produces. The LASSO method was originally introduced in geophysics literature in 1986, and later independently rediscovered and popularized in 1996 by Robert Tibshirani, who used the term and provided further insights into the observed performance. The LASSO method was originally formulated for least squares models and later revealed a substantial amount about the behavior of the estimator and its relationship to ridge regression.

Elastic Net

The elastic net is a regularized regression method that linearly combines the L1 and L2 penalties of the LASSO and ridge methods. Elastic net regularization method includes both LASSO (L1) and Ridge (L2) regularization methods. Overfitting is the core idea behind ML algorithms; the goal is to build models that can find generalized trends within the data. Regularization is used to prevent overfitting the model to training data.

Least Angle Regression

Least angle regression is an algorithm for fitting linear regression models to high-dimensional data. This method was developed by Bradley Efron, Trevor Hastie, Iain Johnstone, and Robert Tibshirani. This statistical algorithm uses a linear combination of a subset of potential covariates to determine a response variable. The least angle regression algorithm produces an estimate of which variables to include, as well as their coefficients. Instead of giving a vector result, this estimate provides a curve that denotes the solution for each value of the L1 norm of the parameter vector. The algorithm is like forward stepwise regression, but instead of including variables at each step, the estimated parameters are increased in a direction equiangular to each one's correlations with the residual.

Rule System

A rule system is often referred to as a rule-based system based on the use of "if-then-else" rule statements. The rules are simply patterning, and an inference engine is used to search for patterns in the rules that match patterns in the data. A matching rule captures a matching process. This process can be used to select and add matches to the rule to apply in the future.

Cubist

The tree-based cubist model can be used to develop an ensemble classifier using a scheme called "committees." The concept of committees is similar to boosting. Both concepts develop a series of trees sequentially with adjusted weights; however, the final prediction is the simple average of predictions from all committee members, which is an idea closer to bagging.

One Rule

One rule is sometimes referred to as one in ten rule. It is a rule of thumb for how many predictor parameters can be estimated during regression analysis (proportional hazards models in survival analysis and logistic regression) while keeping the risk of overfitting low. The rule states that one predictive variable can be studied for every 10 events.

Zero Rule

The zero rule is the simplest classification method that relies on the target and ignores all predictors. The zero rule classifier predicts the majority category (class). For example, if a sample of 300 patients are studied and 20 patients die during the study, the one in ten rule implies that two prespecified predictors can be reliably fitted to the total data. Similarly, if 100 patients die during the study, 10 prespecified predictors can be fitted reliably. If more are fitted, the rule implies that overfitting is likely and the results will not predict well outside the training data. The 1:10 rule is not often violated in fields with many variables, which decreases the confidence in reported findings.

Repeated Incremental Pruning to Produce Error Reduction

In ML, repeated incremental pruning to produce error reduction is a propositional rule learner proposed by William W. Cohen.

Bayesian

Bayesian algorithms involve statistical methods that assign probabilities, distributions, or parameters such as a population mean based on experience or best guesses before experimentation and data collection. Bayesian algorithms apply Bayes' theorem to revise the probabilities and distributions after obtaining experimental data. Bayesian methods are those that explicitly apply Bayes' theorem for problems such as classification and regression.

The most popular Bayesian algorithms are:

- Naive Bayes
- Gaussian Naive Bayes
- Multinomial Naive Bayes
- Averaged one-dependence estimators
- Bayesian belief network
- Bayesian network

Bernoulli Naive Bayes is the other model used in calculating probabilities. A Naive Bayes model is easy to build. It has no complicated iterative parameter estimation, which makes it particularly useful for very large datasets.

Naive Bayes classifier is based on Bayes' theorem with the independence assumptions between predictors; in other words, it assumes that the presence of a feature in a class is unrelated to any other features even if these features depend on each other or upon the existence of the other features. Thus, the name Naive Bayes. See the formula:

$$p(class \mid data) = \frac{P(data \mid class) * P(class)}{P(data)}$$

Gaussian Naive Bayes is used for classification based on the binomial distribution data.

- P(class|data) is the posterior probability of class (target) given predictor (attribute). The probability of a data point having either class, given the data point. This is the value being calculated.

- P(class) is the prior probability of class. This is our prior belief.
- P(data|class) is the likelihood of the probability of predictor given class. This is Gaussian because this is a normal distribution.
- P(data) is the prior probability of predictor or marginal likelihood. This is not calculated in the Naïve Bayes classifiers.

See example Figure 2.9.
See example calculation below:
Steps:

1. *Calculate Prior Probability*
   P(class) = Number of data points in the class/total no. of observations
   P(yellow) = 10/17
   P(green) = 7/17
2. *Calculate Marginal Likelihood*

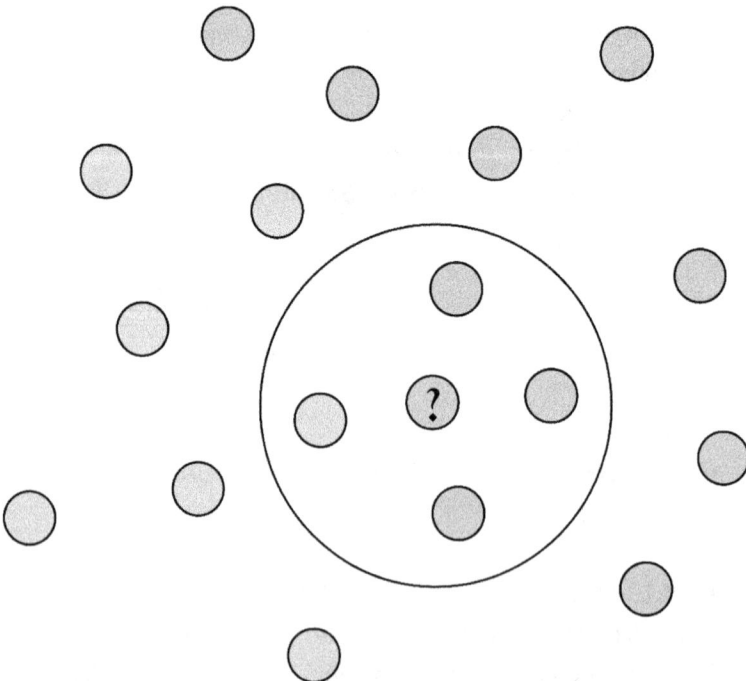

Figure 2.9 Example classification

P(data) = Number of data points similar to observation/total no. of observations

$P(?) = 4/17$

The value is present in checking both the probabilities.

3. Calculate Likelihood

P(data/class) = Number of similar observations to the class/total no. of points in the class.

$P(?/yellow)=1/7$

$P(?/green)=3/10$

4. Posterior Probability for Each Class

5. Classification

P(class1/data)>P(class2/data)

P(green/?)>P(yellow/?)

$$p(class \mid data) = \frac{P(data \mid class) * P(class)}{P(data)}$$

$$P(yellow \mid ?) = \frac{1/7 * 7/17}{4/17} = 0.25$$

$$P(green \mid ?) = \frac{3/10 * 10/17}{4/17} = 0.75$$

The higher probability will be assigned to the class of the category. The calculation shows a 75 percent probability, which is the green class.

Naive Bayes

The Bernoulli Naive Bayes classifier assumes that all the features are binary and take only two values (e.g., a nominal categorical feature that has been one-hot encoded). It is a supervised ML algorithm that uses the Bayes' theorem and assumes that features are statistically independent.

Naïve Bayesian Classifier

Naive Bayes classifiers are a family of simple probabilistic classifiers derived by applying Bayes' theorem with strong (naive) independence assumptions between the features. Naive Bayes has been around since early 1960; however, it used a different name. It was also used for the text retrieval community in early 1960. It is a popular baseline method for text categorizations and the problem of judging documents as belonging to one category or the other (such as spam or legitimate, sports or politics) with word frequencies as the features. This is a good method for risk and security application. This method is popular when combined with more advanced methods such as support vector machines.

It is important to note that Naive Bayes classifiers are highly scalable and require several parameters in the number of variables in a learning problem. Maximum likelihood training can be done by evaluating a closed-form expression that takes linear time, rather than using expensive iterative approximation. Naive Bayes classifier models are widely used in statistics and computer science.

Averaged One-Dependence Estimators

The averaged one-dependence estimators is a probabilistic classification learning technique and is considered the most effective Naive Bayes algorithm. This technique addresses the attribute independence assumption of Naive Bayes by averaging all the dependence estimators.

Bayesian Belief Network

A Bayesian Belief Network or Bayesian Network is a statistical model used to describe the conditional dependencies between different random variables. A Bayesian network is a tool for modeling and reasoning with uncertain beliefs. A Bayesian network consists of two parts: a qualitative component in the form of a directed acyclic graph and a quantitative component in the form with conditional probabilities.

Gaussian Naive Bayes

The Naive Bayes classifier technique is based on the Bayesian theorem and is appropriate when the dimensionality of the inputs is high. The approach is called "naïve" because it assumes the independence between the various attribute values. Naive Bayes assumes label attributes such as binary, categorical, or nominal. A Gaussian distribution is assumed if the input variables are real valued. The algorithm will perform better if the univariate distributions of your data are Gaussian or near-Gaussian.

Multinomial Naive Bayes

The Naive Bayes classifier is a general term, which refers to conditional independence of each of the features in the model. A Multinomial Naive Bayes classifier is a specific instance of a Naive Bayes classifier, which uses a multinomial distribution for each of the features. The multinomial Naive Bayes is used for NLP problems. Naive Bayes is a family of algorithms that applies Bayes theorem with a strong, naive assumption that every feature is independent of the others to predict the category of a given sample.

Bayesian Network

The Bayesian network represents the causal probabilistic relationship among a set of random variables and their conditional dependencies. The network provides a compact representation of a joint probability distribution using a marked cyclic graph. By using a directed graphical model, Bayesian network describes random variables and conditional dependencies. For example, you can use a Bayesian network for a patient suffering from a disease.

Decision Tree

Decision tree analysis is a general, predictive modeling tool that has applications spanning several different areas. Decision trees are constructed using an algorithmic approach that identifies ways to split a dataset based on different conditions. It is one of the most widely used and practical methods for supervised learning. Decision trees are a nonparametric supervised learning method used for both classification and regression tasks. The goal is to create a model that predicts the value of a target variable by learning simple decision rules inferred from the data features. It is a tree-like graph with nodes representing the place to pick an attribute and ask a question. The edges represent the answers to the question, and the leaves represent the actual output or class label. It is used in nonlinear decision making with simple linear decision surface.

Advantages:

1. Decision tree yield is extremely straightforward. It does not require any measurable learning to peruse and decipher decision trees. The graphical portrayal is natural and clients can undoubtedly relate their speculation.
2. Decision trees require less information cleaning contrasted with some other demonstrating systems. Decision trees are not strongly affected by exceptions and missing qualities.
3. Decision trees are viewed as a nonparametric technique. This implies that choice trees have no suspicions about the space appropriation and the classifier structure.

Disadvantages:

1. Overfitting is a common problem with choice tree models. This issue can be addressed by setting requirements on model parameters and pruning (examined in nitty-gritty beneath).
2. Choices trees are not fit for consistent factors. The choice tree loses data when it arranges factors in various classes.

Classification and Regression Tree

Classification and regression trees were introduced by Leo Breiman to refer to the decision tree algorithms used for classification or regression predictive modeling problems. Regression trees are needed when the response variable is numeric or continuous. The target variable determines the type of decision tree needed. In a standard classification tree, the idea is to split the dataset based on the consistency of data.

Iterative Dichotomiser 3 (ID3)

ID3 uses entropy and information gain to construct a decision tree. The decision tree is built top-down from a root node and involves partitioning the data into subsets that contain instances with similar values. The ID3 algorithm uses entropy to calculate the homogeneity of a sample. Entropy in ML uses the information theory to define the certainty of a decision (1 if completely certain and 0 if completely uncertain) as entropy, a probability-based measure used to calculate the amount of uncertainty.

C4.5

The C4.5 is an algorithm used to generate a decision tree. This algorithm was developed by Ross Quinlan. C4.5 is an extension of Quinlan's earlier ID3 algorithm. The decision trees generated by C4.5 can be used for classification; for this reason, C4.5 is often referred to as a statistical classifier.

C5.0

The C5.0 is like C4.5; however, the C5.0 has these features:

- Speed: C5.0 is significantly faster than C4.5 (several orders of magnitude).
- Memory usage: C5.0 is more memory efficient than C4.5.
- Smaller decision trees: C5.0 gets similar results to C4.5 with considerably smaller decision trees.
- Support for boosting: Boosting improves the trees and gives them more accuracy.
- Weighting: C5.0 allows you to weight different cases and misclassification types.
- Winnowing: C5.0 can automatically use winnows algorithms to remove attributes for those that may be unhelpful.

Chi-Square Automatic Interaction Detection

The chi-square automatic interaction detector was created by Gordon V. Kass in 1980. This tool is used to discover the relationship between variables. The detectors' analysis builds a predictive model to determine how variables best merge to explain the outcome in the given dependent variable. A decision tree is drawn upside down with its root at the top. The image on the left uses bold text in black to represent a condition or internal node based on how the tree splits into branches. Decision tree algorithms are generally referred to as classification and regression trees.

Decision Stump

A decision stump is a ML model consisting of a one-level decision tree. The decision tree has one internal node (the root) that is immediately connected to the terminal nodes (the leaves). A decision stump makes a prediction based on the value of a single input feature. Decision stumps are often termed as "weak learners" or "base learners" in ML ensemble techniques such as bagging and boosting. A typical example is the state-of-the-art face detection algorithm that employs AdaBoost with decision stumps as weak learners.

Conditional Decision Trees

Conditional decision trees or conditional inference trees are often referred to as unbiased recursive partitioning is a nonparametric class of decision trees. These trees use a statistical theory (selection by permutation-based significance tests) to select variables instead of selecting the variable that maximizes an information measure.

Dimensionality Reduction

The dimension reduction methods come in unsupervised and supervised forms. Unsupervised methods include the SVD and PCA that use only the matrix of features by samples as well as clustering.

SVD

The SVD of a matrix A is the factorization of A into the product of three matrices $A = UDV\ T$ where the columns of U and V are orthonormal and the matrix D is diagonal with positive real entries. The SVD is useful in many tasks, such as computing the pseudoinverse, least squares fitting of data, multivariable control, matrix approximation, and determining the rank, range, and null space of a matrix. SVD is one of the most widely used unsupervised learning algorithms. SVD is at the center of many recommendation and dimensionality reduction systems for global companies such as Google, Netflix, Facebook, and YouTube.

PCA

PCA explains the variance–covariance structure of a set of variables through linear combinations. The principal component has the largest possible variance in this transformation. PCA is a dimensionality reduction method frequently used to reduce the dimensionality of large datasets. This is done by transforming a large set of variables into a smaller set that still contains most of the information in the large set. Reducing the number of variables of a dataset can lead to a decrease in accuracy; however, the trick in dimensionality reduction is to trade a little accuracy for simplicity. Smaller datasets are easier to explore and visualize, and make analyzing data much easier for ML algorithms. PCA tends to reduce the number of variables of a dataset with much of the information preserved.

Partial Least Squares (PLS) Regression

PLS regression reduces the predictors to a smaller set of uncorrelated components and performs least squares regression on these components instead of the original data. PLS regression is useful when the predictors are highly collinear. This technique is ideal when there are more predictors than observations and if the ordinary least-squares regression either produces coefficients with high standard errors or fails. PLS does not assume that the predictors are fixed, unlike multiple regression. This means that the predictors can be measured with error, making PLS more robust when measuring uncertainty.

Sammon Mapping

Sammon mapping is an algorithm that maps a high-dimensional space to a space of lower dimensionality by preserving the structure of inter-point distances in high-dimensional space in the lower dimension projection. It is particularly suited for use in exploratory data analysis. Sammon mapping was created by John W. Sammon in 1969. It is considered a nonlinear approach, as the mapping cannot be represented as a linear combination of the original variables, which makes Sammon mapping difficult to use with classification applications.

Multidimensional Scaling

Multidimensional scaling is a means of visualizing the level of similarity of individual cases in a dataset. This technique is used to translate information about the pairwise distances among a set of n objects or individuals into a configuration of n points mapped into an abstract Cartesian space.

Projection Pursuit

Projection pursuit is a statistical technique that finds the most interesting projections in multidimensional data. Often, the projections that deviate more from a normal distribution are more interesting.

Principal Component Regression

The principal component regression is a regression analysis technique that originated from PCA. It considers regressing the outcome (predictions) on a set of covariates (also known as predictors, explanatory variables, or independent variables) based on a standard linear regression model and uses PCA for estimating the unknown regression coefficients in the model. Principal component regression helps overcome the multicollinearity problem that arises when two or more of the explanatory variables are close to being collinear. This can be useful in settings with high-dimensional covariates. Through appropriate selection of the principal components, PCR can lead to the efficient prediction of the outcome based on the assumed model.

PLS Discriminant Analysis (PLS-DA)

The PLS-DA is an adaptable algorithm that can be used for predictive and descriptive modeling for discriminative variable selection in ML. Many users have yet to grasp the essence of constructing a valid and reliable PLS-DA model. PLS-DA is a variant used when the Y is categorical. PLS is used to find the fundamental relations between two matrices (X and Y). This technique is a latent variable approach to modeling the covariance structures in these two spaces.

Mixture Discriminant Analysis

The mixture discriminant analysis is a technique used to analyze the research data when the criterion or the dependent variable is categorical and when the predictor or the independent variable is an interval in nature. Discriminant analysis is a classification problem where two or more groups, clusters, or populations are known a priori, and one or more new observations are classified into one of the known populations based on the measured characteristics.

Quadratic Discriminant Analysis (QDA)

The QDA for nominal labels and numerical attributes determines which variables discriminate between two or more naturally occurring groups. This technique also determines whether the variables have a descriptive or a predictive objective. The QDA may also refer to qualitative data analysis when used in qualitative research. The QDA extension is used for quadruple discriminant archives. QDA is used in statistical classification or used as a quadratic classifier in ML.

Regularized Discriminant Analysis

Regularized discriminant analysis is a method that generalizes various class-conditional Gaussian classifiers, including linear discriminant analysis, QDA, and Gaussian Naive Bayes. The linear discriminant analysis method offers a continuum between these models by tuning two hyper-parameters that control the amount of regularization applied to the estimated covariance matrices. Linear discriminant analysis is the most commonly used classification method for movement intention decoding from myoelectric signals.

AI and ML Process Steps

The AI process steps are shown in Figure 2.10. It is important that you follow the steps carefully to understand the processes that are required (Shrestha et al. 2019).

Data Processing

The data processing step is used with any data projects. Please refer to the data processing section of this chapter.

Model

The model step determines which model fits for the AI and ML problem definitions as well as the use case. Use the selecting approach appropriately to model the prioritization and evaluation.

Refer to the chapter on ML algorithms.

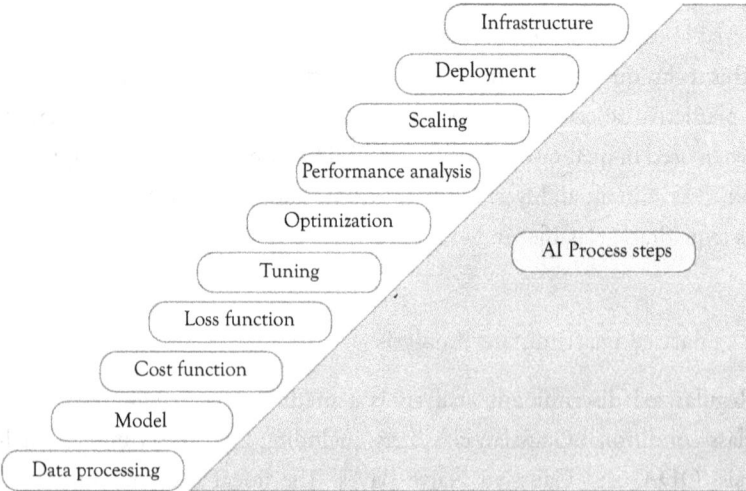

Figure 2.10 AI process steps

Cost Function

Cost function helps correct and change behavior to minimize mistakes. Cost function measures how wrong the model is in terms of its ability to estimate the relationship between predicted value versus actual value. The goal of the cost function is to minimize the differences between predicted versus actual. The gradient descent optimization algorithm is commonly used.

Loss Function

Loss function evaluates how well the algorithm models predict using the given data and analyzes how the model is improving. If the loss function returns a higher number, the model is ineffective. If the loss function is minimized, the model is improving.

Different types of loss functions are mean squared error, likelihood functions, log loss, and cross entropy loss.

Tuning

Tuning is a crucial step to improve accuracy and adjust the model by tuning hyperparameters, applying proper regularization, avoiding overfitting and underfitting, bootstrapping, cross-validation, and bagging. See Figure 2.11.

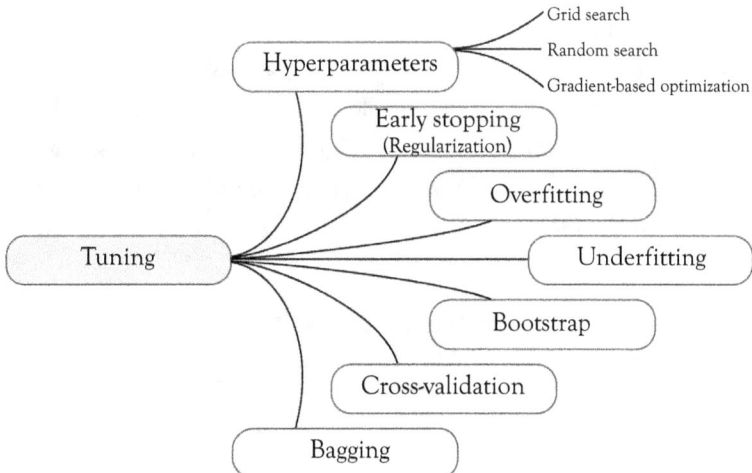

Figure 2.11 ML model tuning steps

A major challenge in this step is how quickly tunings can be applied to improve accuracy and reduce the loss.

Optimization

An optimization is a procedure that is executed iteratively by comparing various solutions until an optimum or a satisfactory solution is found. When optimizing a design, the objective is to minimize the cost and loss and to maximize the efficiency.

Updating model parameters such as weights and bias values and determining Gradient descent, Stochastic gradient descent, or Adam can provide faster results.

Optimization algorithms help to minimize or maximize an objective function (also referred to as an Error function) E(x), which is a mathematical function dependent on the model's internal learnable parameters that are used when computing the target values (Y) from the set of predictors (X). Optimization also determines adjustments of weight (W) and bias (b) values and determines the learning rate. First-order optimization algorithms and second-order optimization algorithms are most commonly used.

Gradient descent is the most important technique and the foundation of how to train and optimize intelligent system. The batch gradient descent calculates the gradient of the whole dataset and performs the update only once. This process can be very slow with large datasets. The speed is determined by the learning rate—η and is guaranteed to converge to global minimum rather than local minimum, whereas Stochastic gradient descent performs an update for each training dataset. Mini-batch gradient descent encompasses the best of both techniques and performs an update for every batch with n training examples in each batch.

Performance Analysis

The performance analysis step evaluates the performance of the model and determines the next step that must be taken to improve the accuracy and reduce the error or loss. This step also determines the parameters that need to be adjusted for optimal performance on the picked models and

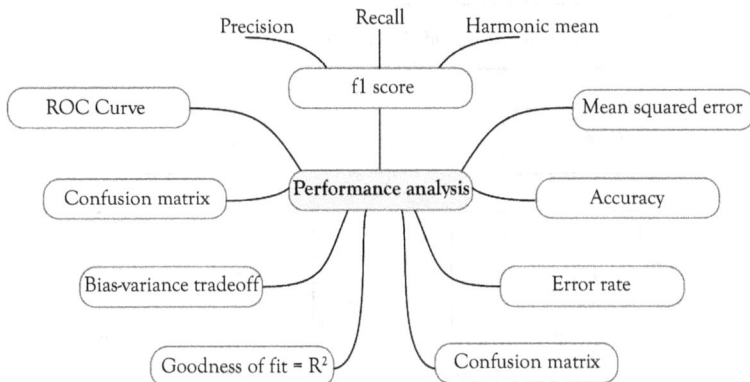

Figure 2.12 Performance analysis

before the models are scaled up to large training datasets and enabled for continues learning using the AL and ML process. The next step is to review how to scale up or down to handle a large volume of training data and how to enable automatic learning and predict outcomes using new arrival datasets.

See Figure 2.12.

See Figure 2.13.

ML Use Case Mind Map

See Figure 2.14.

Critical Measures:

- Net present value (NPV)
- ROI
- Internal rate of return (IRR)
- Payback period (PBP)
- Benefit–cost ratio (BCR)

Critical Measures for Startups and Project Management

NPV is a value in the form of a sum of money rather than a future value it would become when invested at compound interest. For example, $220

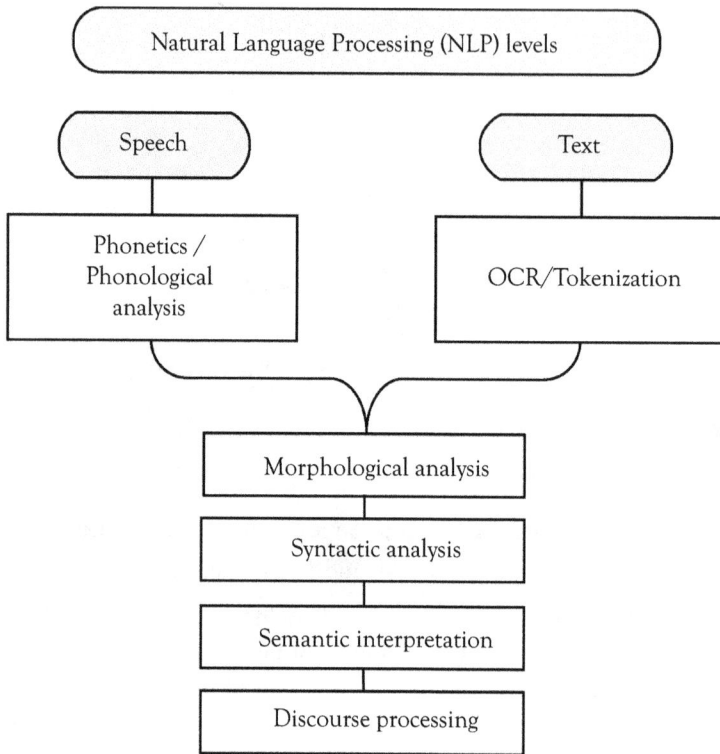

Figure 2.13 NLP steps on how the natural languages process is typically processed

due in 12 months' time has a present value of $200 today if invested at an annual rate of 10 percent.

ROI measures the gain or loss generated on an organization investment related to the amount invested. The ROI is usually expressed as a percentage and is used for personal financial decisions to compare a company's profitability to different investments.

The ROI formula is:

ROI = (Net Profit/Cost of Investment) × 100

The ROI calculation is flexible and has various uses. It can be used to calculate and compare potential investments or an investor could use it to calculate the return on a stock.

The IRR is a metric used in capital budgeting to estimate profit of a potential investment. The IRR is a discount rate that makes the NPV of

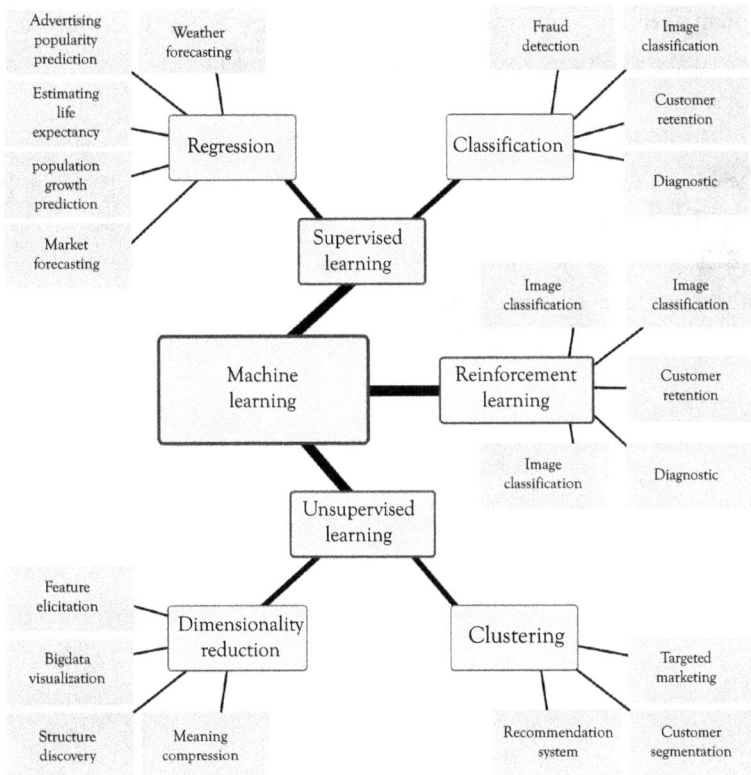

Figure 2.14 ML use case map on how algorithms map to use cases

all cash flows from a project equal to zero. IRR calculations rely on the same formula as NPV does.

NPV is the difference between the present value of cash inflows and the present value of cash outflows over a period. The NPV is used for capital budgeting and investment planning to analyze the profit of a projected investment or project.

The PBP is the length of time required to pay back an investment. The payback period of a given investment or project can determine whether to undertake the position or project. If the payback is long, the project may not be desirable for the investment. The payback period does not consider the time value of money. Other formulas such as NPV, IRR, and discounted cash flow consider payback periods.

The time value of money or present discounted value means the current value of money has more value than the future value due to its potential earning capacity. This core principle of finance maintains that provided money can earn interest; any amount of money is worth more the sooner it is received.

The BCR is used as an indicator in cost–benefit analysis to determine the relationship between the relative costs and benefits of a proposed project. This is expressed in monetary or qualitative terms. If a project has a BCR greater than 1.0, the project is assumed to deliver a positive net present value to an investment.

CHAPTER 3

Knowledge Base

Chapter Outline

- Define knowledge base for the artificial intelligence (AI) project
- Risk and security knowledge development
- Objectives of the risk and security knowledge base
- Identification of knowledge for risk and security
- Knowledge acquisition for risk and security
- Knowledge sharing

Key Learning Points

- Learn and understand knowledge base
- Understand risk and security knowledge base development

AI can be used repeatedly in applications with different needs. Human resources has been tough for organizations, and organizations have attempted to capture and use the human intelligence required for different roles. The captured knowledge and intelligence are stored in the knowledge base. Knowledge models can be built, trained, and used when necessary.

Capturing human intelligence requires an integrated information system. The idea is to develop an integrated system that can provide the knowledge required by human experts. These integrated systems should be readily available and sharable. The integrated system should be used with strategic objectives in mind. This leads to the development of AI.

AI solves important challenges based on the information stored in the knowledge base. Human experts have cyclical demands in their subject matter expertise. Similar approaches are applied to risk management and are explored with use cases.

The knowledge base stores data, techniques, and algorithms that are used to drive the AI-integrated system. The integrated system will be introduced gradually in the approach. The objective of the AI-integrated system is to seek mitigation solutions to risk and security in corporate settings. The objectives will consider using business rules that consist of "what if" questions. This approach will use strategic rules and logic to determine possible mitigation solutions to risk and security using the stored data in the knowledge base. The AI-integrated system will impact setting knowledge objectives, identification of knowledge, knowledge acquisition, knowledge development, knowledge sharing, preservation of knowledge, fixing of knowledge, use of knowledge, evaluation of knowledge, and measurement of knowledge. Integration of AI case-based knowledge, representation of risk and security cases, identification of similarities, and connection are the building blocks of the knowledge base. Bizstats.ai uses the knowledge base to build AI-integrated systems from scratch.

Risk and Security Knowledge Development

The purpose of this section is to generate the risk and security knowledge required. This will include ideas, models, skills, processes, and system methods. Machine learning (ML) can have various forms. Pattern-based learning will be used when discussing ML and neural networks. This method provides appropriate knowledge from a large amount of risk and security data, enabling change of behavior of the captured data in the AI system.

Objectives of the Risk and Security Knowledge Base

Skills and knowledge will be developed using appropriate corporate objectives in the Bizstats.ai risk and security knowledge base.

The objectives of the risk knowledge base are as follows:

- To capture the risks and associated risks from the data, process, people, Internet of Things (IoT), systems, and actions.

- To determine occurrence.
- To determine impact of risks.
- To determine risk priority.
- To allocate risk owner.
- To determine risk mitigation.
- To determine risk action.
- To risk continuously in real-time and determine corrective actions.

The objectives of security knowledge base:

- To capture the threat and associated security risks from the data, process, people, IoT, systems, and actions.
- To determine threat occurrence.
- To determine impact of threats.
- To determine security threat priority.
- To allocate security owner.
- To determine security mitigation.
- To determine security action.
- To monitor security threat(s) continuously in real-time and determine corrective action.
- To recommend security training and efficient security process(s).

Identification of Knowledge for Risk and Security

The corporate setting will be used to model the skills and knowledge that enables AI to work well. This will require mapping the risk and security knowledge. Every effort will be made to store the data in a form that enables the data to be retrieved correctly. This AI system will allow access to the collected data. Ultimately, the system should build a corporate knowledge base capable of being extended with new risk and security data. The AI system will prevent any loss of information, retain information, and keep the risk and security data up to date. The system will automatically be capable of building the knowledge base, and additional information can be accessed externally.

Knowledge Acquisition for Risk and Security

Risk and security data will be collected using formal and informal channels. The data will be used internally and externally and will enable suitable competencies of the AI system. The data will ultimately be used with statistical, ML algorithms.

Knowledge Sharing

Risk and security knowledge sharing is a critical part of the knowledge management cycle. It is important to realize that people, technology, and the corporate world are part of this phase. AI knowledge sharing solutions consist of machine intelligence that is capable of learning from other AI systems through real-time connectivity using real-time application programming interfaces. It has been proven that discovering trends in a specific area such as risk and security mitigation can be effective. Another area where AI has been used efficiently is the vehicle manufacturing industry. Humans do not need to go through the repetitive nature of using the data; the computer system does the job efficiently without overwhelming. Bizstats.ai has access to real-time application programming interfaces to solve knowledge sharing problems.

CHAPTER 4

Root Cause Analytics and Analysis

Determine the root cause of the identified risk and the analytics and analysis that will be used.

Root Cause Analytics and Analysis Details

Each identified risk will be allocated to the risk owner.

The risk owner must research the risk thoroughly for root cause analysis to gain detailed knowledge of the risk and the causes.

Root cause analysis and analytics requires complete human interaction to enable in-depth analysis.

Risk Mitigation Strategy Recommendation

Risk Mitigation Strategies:

- Assume and accept
  o Acknowledge the existence of a particular risk and make a deliberate decision to accept it without engaging in special efforts to control it. Approval of project or program leaders is required.
- Avoid
  o Adjust program requirements or constraints to eliminate or reduce the risk. This adjustment could be accommodated by a change in funding, scheduling, or technical requirements.
- Control
  o Implement actions to minimize the impact or likelihood of risk.

- Transfer
  - o Reassign organizational accountability, responsibility, and authority to another stakeholder willing to accept the risk.
- Watch and monitor
  - o Monitor the environment for changes that affect the nature and the impact of the risk.

CHAPTER 5

Recommendation Engine

The recommendation engine illustrates the logical flow as shown in Figure 5.1. Recommendation engines recommend strategies for risk mitigation and risk contingency.

Data Collection

Gathering risk data starts with the data collection process shown in Tables 5.1, 5.2, 5.3, and 5.4 (Hahn 2018; Elswick 2016; Phillips and Stawarski 2008).

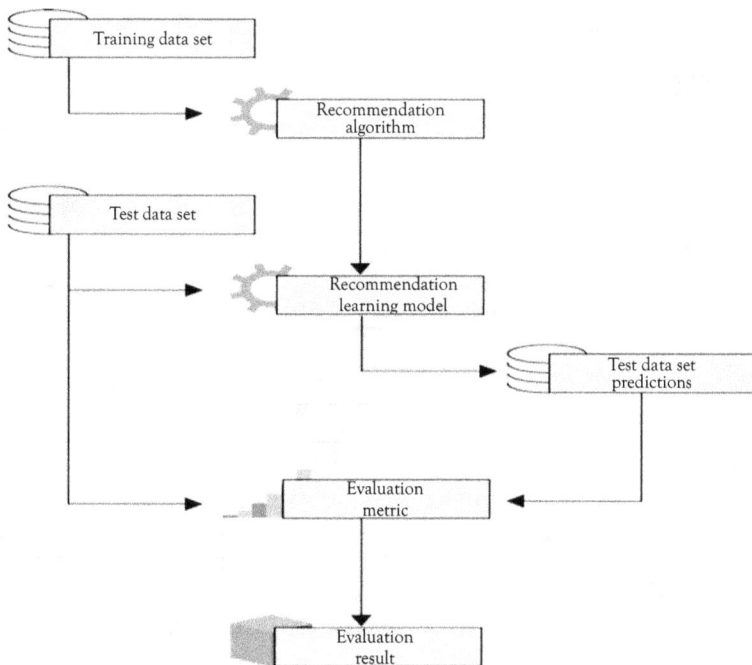

Figure 5.1 Recommendation engine

Table 5.1 Risks dataset

Measure Risk Name	Risk Category	Risk Impact Score	Risk Occurrence Probability	Risk Priority Score
Sales amount decrease	Financial/competitive risk	0.9	0.5	2
Inventory turnover decrease	Inventory risk	0.2	0.8	9
Inventory decrease	Inventory risk			
Sales amount increase	Inventory risk			

Table 5.2 Risk mitigation strategies dataset

Measure Risk Name	Risk Mitigation Strategy	# of Times Mitigation Strategy Taken	# of Times Mitigation Strategy Taken/# of Times Measure Risk Occurred
Sales amount decrease	Encourage customers to increase spending with your company	10	0.9
Inventory turnover decrease	Revise business strategy	20	0.3
Inventory decrease	Performance-based contracts with suppliers		
Sales amount increase	Improve forecasting models		

Table 5.3 Interaction matrix

Risk Mitigation Strategy	Mitigation Type
Run new marketing campaign	Avoid
Increase inventory	Avoid
Discontinue product	Control
Acquire new customers	Capture
Keep current customers happy	Maintain
Encourage customers to increase spending with your company	Grow
Win back former customers	Reclaim
Revise business strategy	Control
Performance-based contracts with suppliers	Control
Improve forecasting models	Control

Table 5.4 Risk-security strategies

Risk/Mitigation Strategy	Run New Marketing Campaign	Decrease Inventory	Revise Business Strategy	Performance-Based Contracts With Suppliers	Improve Forecasting Models
Sales amount decrease	5 (# of times taken this strategy)	0	2	0	1
Inventory turn-over decrease	1	5	3	0	1
Inventory decrease	0	0	0	4	0
Sales amount increase	0	0	0	0	5

Design Algorithm

Recommendation engines can be designed based on risk–risk similarity models or mitigation-strategy similarity models.

Identify List of Recommender System Algorithms

Machine learning (ML) algorithms in recommender systems:

- Content-based filtering methods (similarity of item attributes).
- Collaborative-based filtering methods (calculates similarity from interactions, risk–risk, or mitigation strategy similarity models):
  o K: nearest neighbors.
  o Matrix factorization: stochastic gradient descent.
  o Matrix factorization: alternating least squares.
  o Association rules: Apriori algorithm (items frequently consumed together are connected with an edge in the graph).
  o Neural networks.
- Deep autoencoder—with multiple hidden layers and nonlinearities that are more powerful but harder to train—can be

used to preprocess item attributes and combine content-based and collaborative approaches.

- Neural nets predict ratings and interactions based on item and user attributes.
- Deep neural nets predict next action based on historical actions and content.
- Deep autoencoders: collaborative filtering.
- Ensemble of deep and wide regression to predict ratings.
- Sequence-based recommenders can be realized by traditional ML models.
- Gated Recurrent Units or Long Short-Term Memory (LSTM) recurrent neural networks.
- Deep convolutional neural networks.
- Feed-forward neural nets with history of purchases on-hot-encoded to input predicting probabilities of products to be purchased next.
- Combination of both.
- Finalized.
  o Train the model using collaborative-based filtering methods.

Train the Model

Training set (80 percent) and testing set (20 percent).

The testing set is further divided into an observation subset that is submitted to the system and the testing subset is used to evaluate the system.

Evaluate the Model

- Evaluated similarly to a classification ML model.
- Root mean squared error.

See Figures 5.2, 5.3, and 5.4.

Introduce regularization parameters to all algorithms to penalize recommendation of popular items.

k- Nearest neighbors

Association rules

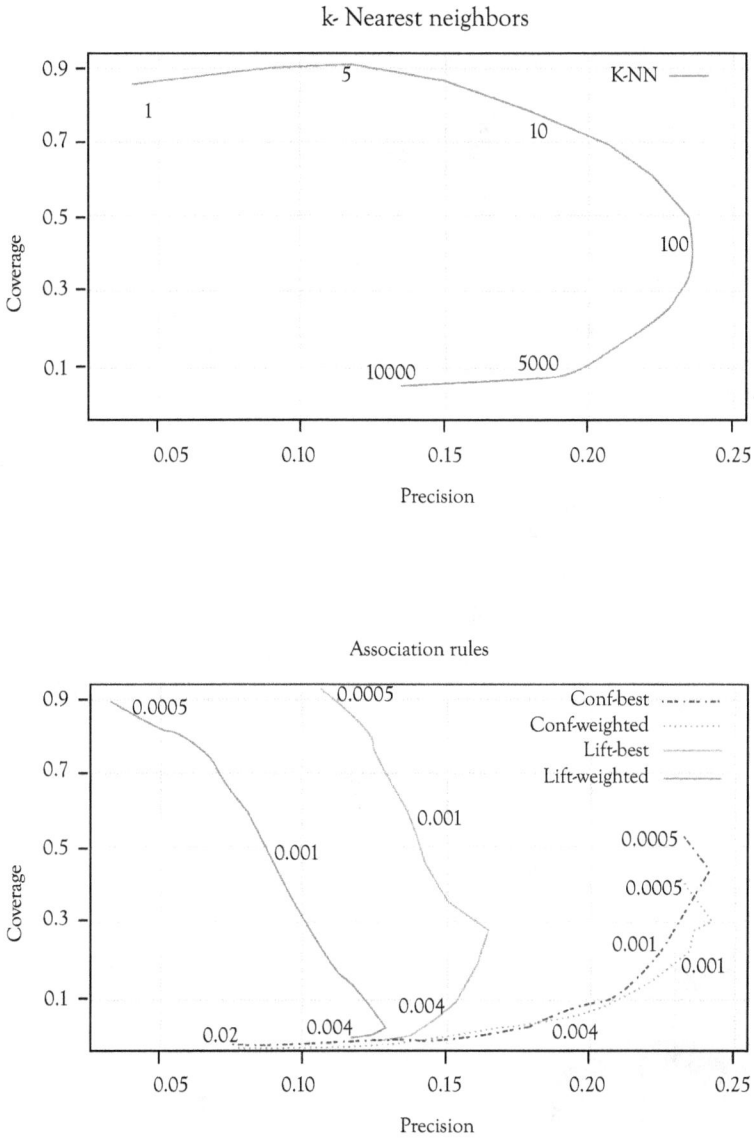

Figure 5.2 K-Nearest neighbors and association rules

- Both recall and coverage should be maximized; recommender will be accurate and give diverse recommendations for users to explore new content.

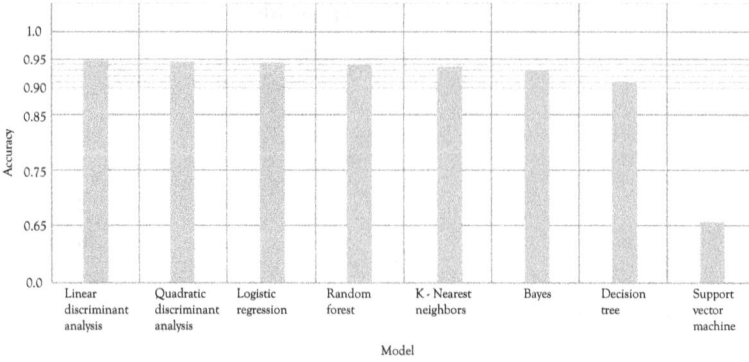

Figure 5.3 Model versus accuracy

- Cold starts do not have enough historical interactions (for item or user). Attribute similarity (content-based similarity) may be used as collaborative filtering methods that fail to generate recommendations.
- Cold start problems are reduced when attribute similarity is taken into account. Encode attributes into the binary vector and feeds it to recommender.
- Items clustered based on their interaction similarity and attribute similarity are often aligned.

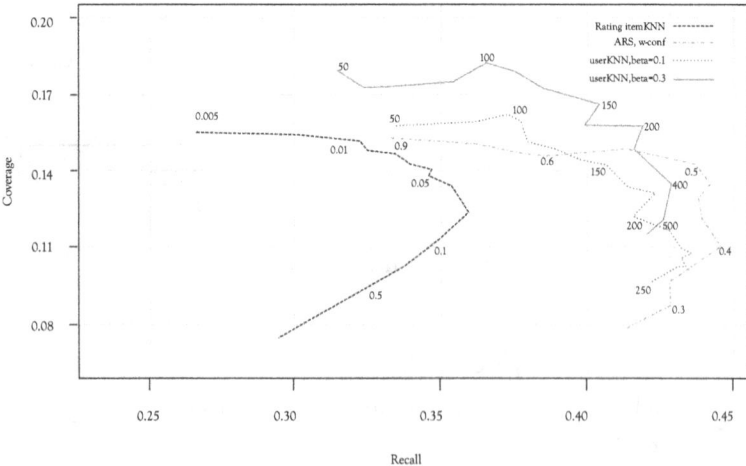

Figure 5.4 Coverage versus recall: Recommendation engine evaluation

Evaluation Metrics for Recommendation Engines

- (a) Recall, (b) what proportion of items that a user likes were actually recommended, and (c) the larger the recall, the better the recommendations.
- (a) Precision, (b) out of all the recommended items, how many did the user actually like?, and (c) the larger the precision, the better the recommendations.
- (a) Root mean squared error, (b) it measures the error in the predicted ratings, and (c) the smaller the root mean squared error value, the better the recommendations.
- (a) Ranking metrics and (b) considers the order of the products recommended:
  - o (a) Mean reciprocal rank, (b) evaluates the list of recommendations, and (c) the larger the mean reciprocal rank, the better the recommendations.
  - o (a) Mean average precision at cutoff k, and (b) the larger the mean average precision, the more accurate the recommendations.
  - o (a) Normalized discounted cumulative gain, and (b) the higher the normalized discounted cumulative gain, the better the recommendations.

See Figures 5.5 and 5.6.

- One algorithm is fine, but ensembles are much more powerful.

		Actual	
		Positive	Negative
Predicted	Positive	True Positive	False Positive
	Negative	False Negative	True Negative

Figure 5.5 Confusion matrix

Setting	Recall
Feed-forward symbols	16.154%
Feed-forward Images	16.186%
LSTM symbols	18.637%
LSTM Images	20.013%
Baseline features k-NN	5.673%
Baseline Interaction k-NN	4.894%
Baseline Bestseller per week	2.384%

Figure 5.6 Evaluation metrics for recommendation engines

- Balance exploration and exploitation because exploring too much can lead to lower quality recommendation for some users, whereas limited exploration can lead to suboptimal recommendations for all users.

Model Conclusion

LSTM performed better than other algorithms for recommendation engine.

Conclusion

Many recommendation engines are available in the market.

Reinforcement Learning (Q-Learning) for Recommendations

Reinforcement learning has been shown to solve complex problems. Recently, reinforcement learning has been used with great success in Google's DeepMind Atari games (Sutton and Barto 1998).

Underlying ML algorithms for Q-Learning do not have restrictions. The model can be any regression algorithms; however, deep neural networks dominate Q-Learning and reinforcement learning in general.

One key difference can be noted when using logistic regression for instead of classification is the data. In classification, the data are prelabeled with the correct class for the model to predict. Reinforcement learning does not have prelabeled data. Data are generated and these data have a reward signal that should be maximized.

Threat Response Recommendations

Suppose a risk is observed and a list of actions are taken. It is fed into the actor network, which decides what would the next action should be. It produces an ideal response embedding. It can be compared with other response embeddings to find similarities. The best match will be recommended for the risk.

The critic helps to judge the actor and help it find out what is wrong.

For example, the recommender suggests an action for a risk. The action was taken and receives an immediate reward of $1,000; however, it may also happen that the action is undone in the future, penalizing the company by $2,000. All future actions need to be taken into consideration. See Figure 5.7.

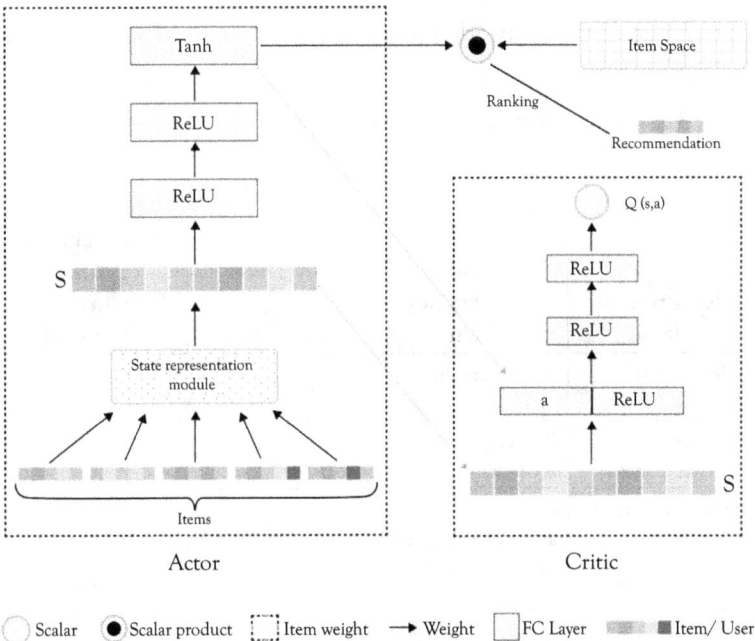

Figure 5.7 *Reinforcement learning algorithm generic process diagram*

The network consists of two layers: the actor and the critic. Each one resembles different learning types. The actor learns policies (probabilities of which action to choose next) and the critic is focused on rewards (Q-Learning).

First, a bunch of response embeddings are fed into the actor's state representation module, where they are encoded. Next, a decision is made in the form of a vector. The action is combined with item embeddings and fed into the critic module, which aims to estimate how good the reward is going to be.

The state module models the complex dynamic risk-response interactions to pursue better recommendation performance.

For a given risk, the network accounts for generating a response is based on its states. The risk state denoted by the embeddings of its n latest response taken is used as the input.

Critic Network (Q-Learning) is used to estimate how good the reward of the current state and action will be.

Four categories of features have been constructed: risk features, context features as the state features of the environment, risk-response features, and response features as the action features. The four features were input to the deep Q-network to calculate the Q-value. A list of responses

Table 5.5 Risk contingency dataset

Measure Risk Name	Risk Contingency Plan	# of Times Contingency Plan Taken	# of Times Contingency Plan Taken/# of Times Measure Risk Occurred
Sales amount decrease	Design new products	10	0.9
Inventory turnover decrease	Reduce price to boost sales	20	0.3
Inventory decrease	Create a list of alternative suppliers for inventory items	5	0.45
Sales amount increase	Fall back on overstocked inventory items	7	0.68

were chosen to recommend based on the Q-value, and the user's action on the response was included in the reward the reinforcement learning agent received.

Rewards can be collected from recommendation engines' system log.

Risk Contingency Recommendation

Recommendation engines are trained using the same steps as the threat response recommendation engine. See Table 5.5.

CHAPTER 6

Functional Domain

Purpose

This chapter describes each of the main business functional areas of major risk and security for the following business functional area:

- Sales and marketing (S&M) functional area
- Customer relationship management (CRM) functional area
- Financial management functional area
- Human resource functional area
- Manufacturing functional area
- Operations management functional area
- Supply chain management (SCM) functional area
- R&D functional area
- Artificial intelligence (AI) and automation functional area

S&M within the functional area

1. Top risks in the area:

S&M is an important business functional area for any business. S&M is the revenue generating functional area. Identifying risk in this area takes higher priority before it hits the revenue and sales. See the following reference:

https://simplicable.com/new/marketing-risk

2. Security in the area:

Chief marketing officer's top security threats

https://cisoinsights.com/top-3-cyber-security-risks-every-chief-marketing-officer-care/

S&M Functional Area

S&M get involved with the operations and activities that promote and sell products and services. The strategy is to sell and distribute products or services. S&M includes research and development of pricing, research, development, distribution, customer service, sales, and communications. Typically, the sales department has an obligation to advise the marketing department with possible customers and focuses.

The marketing department makes the decisions and the sales workforce uses the ideas to sell the products and services. An example could be software products. The sales workforce uses the ideas to sell the software packages. Both the marketing and sales jobs contribute information, ideas, and research to aid with marketing strategies and brainstorm approaches for various products and services that will lead to special promotions, sponsored events, and other ideas.

The coordination between the marketing and sales departments can lead to risk and security issues. At all cost, organizations want to avoid those problems to increase sales and promotions.

CRM Functional Area

CRM is a tool used for contact and sales management. CRM enhances sales and promotes environmental relationships. CRM aids in coining strategic relationships and interactions with customers and potential customers. CRM promotes connection with customers, streamlines processes, and eventually improves an organization's profitability.

Important features of CRM:

Contact management: CRM helps the organization better connect with customers.

Mobility: CRM can access customer data and other important information on the customers.

Analytics: CRM helps refine important actionable items that are defined by the organization.

Customization: The CRM system is customizable to suit the organization in unique situations. A flexible CRM allows synchronization of operating systems that provide full control over the kind of data being used and updates and reevaluates the processes when required.

Simplicity: CRM is simple to use. Employees using the system should embrace it to make it worthwhile. The CRM is easy to understand, intuitive to use, and straightforward in its reports.

The aforementioned features are necessary in order to avoid risk and security issues.

Other CRM risks are as follows:

1. Inappropriate CRM project assumptions that may cause confusion among stakeholders.
2. The project planning was ineffective and left out important parts of the requirements, leading to significant issues.
3. The data conversion is delayed due to problems with data conversion and incorrect data.
4. Incorrect processes are created in inappropriate business processes. Incorrect data added from another location creates confusion or unmatched datasets.
5. Failure to address challenges or risks in the system.
6. Lack of executive support that creates problems in the CRM project environment.
7. The organization perceived the CRM as a surplus application.
8. Inappropriate care of the CRM requirements by the workforce.
9. Users do not use the CRM system appropriately.
10. The risk is not being attended to appropriately.

All identified risks must be mitigated appropriately to keep the environment safe.

Financial Management Functional Area

The financial management areas consist of strategy, marketing, finance, human resources, technology and equipment, and operations.

The primary areas of business finance consist of the following:

- Corporate finance: This area covers the decisions an organization makes about financing.

- Investments: The corporation may decide to invest in assets. These assets may be short-term securities to long-term securities, such as stocks and bonds.
- Financial markets and institutions: The financial markets may include stock and bond markets, the primary and markets, and the money and capital between markets. Financial markets may include the stock market. Financial markets are used to transfer funds saver funds to fund users. Typically, savers are household and users tend to be businesses and the government.

The three areas tend to overlap and tend to cover distinct aspects of finance.

There are risks in financial management, such as an entity making an investment decision that exposes financial risks. The different types of risks in finance are credit risk (i.e., if an organization takes a loan and not able to pay back), liquidity risk, and equity risk (the third type of financial risk).

Financial risks must be assessed completely to determine loss on an asset, loan, or investment. The rate of return needs to be determined and effort must be made for a particular investment to succeed.

Human Resource Functional Area

Human resources manage valuable resources for positions with other organizations. The human resources recruiter recruits new hires, maintains benefits and payroll, mediates conflict, and engages in training and development of new hires. Here are other functions of human resources:

- Employee and labor relations.
- Strategic management.
- Workforce planning and employment that includes recruitment and selection of opportunities.
- Human resource development of new hire employee training and development.
- Ensure that employees are managed well to cut labor costs.

- Protect employee rights and ensure that employees operate within the scope of the employer requirements and regulations.
- Total rewards for employee compensation and benefits.
- Policy formulation for the recruitment organization as well as the client organization.
- Ensure that risk management is done well.

Human resources has two types of risks: production decrease and reduction of human resource. These risks must be mitigated by means of risk management. Typical mitigations are increasing productivity (i.e., strategic planning that minimizes the probability of financial losses) based on excellent leadership (i.e., trust, motivation, planning, delegation of authority, and the development of policies and procedures to document best practices), training (i.e., a systematic approach, patience, and an honest evaluation), communication, evaluation skills, motivation (i.e., motivate the employee), evaluation, and conflict resolution.

Manufacturing Functional Area

The following are some of the risks in the manufacturing functional area:

- Emerging markets can be unpredictable.
- The supply chain has the tendency to be delayed or disrupted for various reasons.
- Third-party vendors caused by a stakeholder who the manufacturing organization is doing business with.
- Information technology is a technology problem and can occur for various reasons.
- Staff management and succession planning can be a problem if not done well.
- Risk can set in and create disruption if the workforce in the manufacturing environment is not proactive.

Here are additional risks in the manufacturing functional area:

- Data collection must be done well on the following items: information regarding inventory, supply, deliveries, quality, production, customer support, processing, and day-to-day management.

- Unexpected catastrophic equipment failures may cause dramatic delays.
- Data collected may be inaccurate.
- Possibility of slow onboarding and knowledge loss due to new employees becoming familiar with the work environment and functionalities.
- Working with machines and new processes can be overwhelming sometimes.

All the risks and security issues can be mitigated appropriately.

Operations Management Functional Area

Operations management ensures the timely outcome of raw material into finished products. It is safe to say that operations management is important when it comes to project management. In an organization, the business function is responsible for planning, organization, coordinating, and controlling the resources required to produce the organization's services and products. High priorities ensure timely delivery of products and services.

Operations management involves similar management for organizational sectors irrespective of the type or nature. The main idea is to properly cater to the resources such as labor, raw material, money, and other resources. Organizations will use available resources in the best possible way to achieve end goals and improve overall productivity. The organization tries to provide products to align with customer requirements. This strategy helps to market and sell the end products rapidly, resulting in enormous profits for the organization. Operations management manages sectors such as design, operations, and maintenance of the system used to produce goods.

The operations management process cannot be underestimated and in-depth knowledge is required. A mishandled environment leads to risk and security issues that impact the organization's growth and success.

The risks of operations management include loss based on personnel, procedures, systems, and external events. Personnel-based risks include personnel who are not trained well and good employees leaving the organization. Operational risk and loss stems from preplanned detrimental activity, such as employees committing criminal offenses that could potentially harm the organization.

Other risks and security issues are:

- Computer hacking.
- Risks coming from disastrous events such as hurricanes.
- Internal and external fraud.
- The workforce not adhering to internal policies.
- IT disruption from disabling cyberattacks, routine causes of human error, or failure of aging hardware.
- Data compromise such as cybertheft, unauthorized access, accidental disclosure, and employee negligence.
- Regulatory risk resulting from the evolving nature of regulatory attitudes to supervision.
- Theft and fraud are part and parcel of a risk manager's job.
- Outsourcing remains one of the top operational risks for practitioners this year.
- The incorrect selling of financial products has been a constant concern for operations risk managers over the past decade.
- The financial industry's struggle to attract, train, and retain the best and brightest in competition from other sectors such as technology.
- Organizational change is pointed out as a huge risk concern.
- Unauthorized trading resulting from rogue algorithms is noted as a risk.
- Model risks reflect the growing regulatory burdens placed on banks' modeling and validation teams that show the potential cost of errors that occur in the banking sector.

All risks and security issues must be well managed and mitigated accurately.

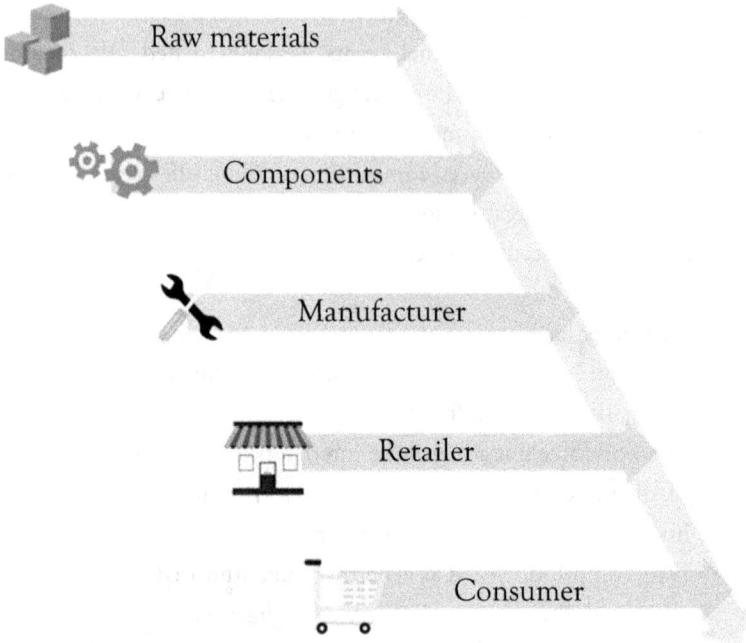

Figure 6.1 **SCM**

SCM

SCM includes the activities required to plan, control, and execute a product's flow, from obtaining raw materials and production through distribution to the final customer (Samson 2010). SCM controls product quality, inventory levels, timing, and expenses. Other examples are farming, refining, design, manufacturing, packaging, and transportation.

Retail organizations often get involved in SCM because product quality is controlled all the way to the end customer. See Figure 6.1.

SCM has risks and needs that must be managed appropriately. The following are some basic types of supply chain risks:

- Financial risks.
- Any unforeseen event that disturbs the normal flow of goods and materials in a supply chain.
- Scope of schedule risks.
- Legal risks.
- Environmental risks.

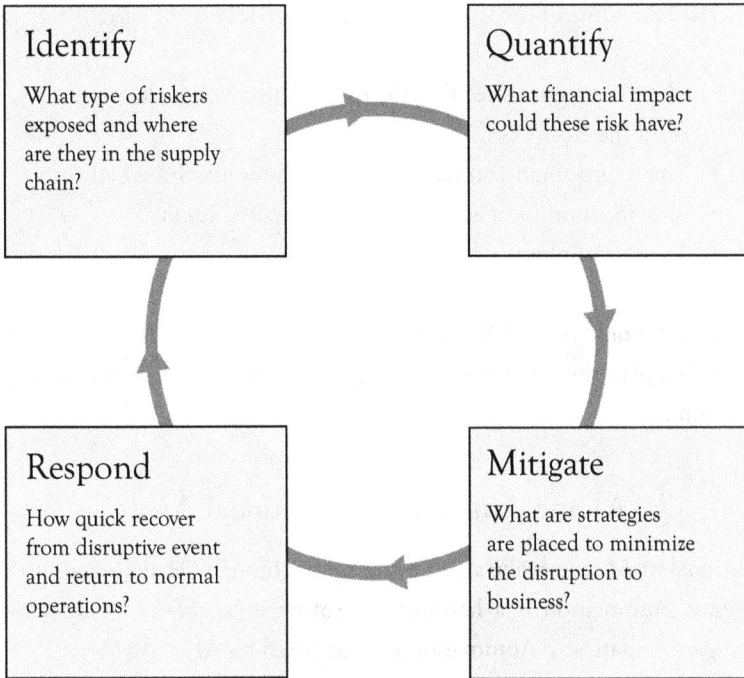

Identify

What type of riskers exposed and where are they in the supply chain?

Quantify

What financial impact could these risk have?

Respond

How quick recover from disruptive event and return to normal operations?

Mitigate

What are strategies are placed to minimize the disruption to business?

Figure 6.2 Supply chain risk management

- Sociopolitical (combining social and political factors) risks.
- Project organization risks.
- Human behavior risks.

The risks in the supply chain must be managed using supply chain risk management (SCRM). The SCRM uses strategic steps to identify, assess, and mitigate the risks embedded in the supply chain process. It is necessary to manage all tiers of supply and risk objects (suppliers, locations, and ports). See Figure 6.2.

R&D

R&D is the process where an organization searches for new knowledge to create new products, services, or systems (Hill et al. 2019). The goal is to make money for the organization. Pharmaceutical and technology organizations carry out R&D; however, other types of organizations also use R&D. Usually, R&D is basic or applied in order to acquire new knowledge.

Here are some of the risks associated with R&D:

- There is no guarantee that the organization will make money from the R&D.
- The return on investment could be disappointing.
- The organization may not obtain the desired result.
- The risk of physical harm.

R&D should be well planned and include a detailed risk management plan. The plan should contain contingency in terms of time, scheduling, and funds.

AI and Automation Functional Area

The goal of AI is to make a computer mimic human behavior and intelligence. Automation is a hardware or software capable of doing some things automatically. Automation may be based on AI.

Some fear that in the future, AI, ML, and automation will replace 7 percent of jobs in the United States alone. AI and automation are forecasted to eliminate most routine tasks, freeing IT to think more strategically.

Here are some of the risks of AI and automation:

- Any career with repetitive tasks is a candidate for automation.
- With bots in front lines, it will be increasingly difficult to justify spending money on IT support.

Mitigation or preparation for the game changing:

- Do not resist automation; embrace it.
- Bots can answer common question and point users to frequently asked questions.
- Work on developing skills that will be in high demand in the future.
- Learn to bridge the gap between business and tech-speak; try to look at reality.

- Be valuable to a wide variety of people (mostly customers).
- Take advantage of leadership training opportunities to help your team.
- Be a team player and work with teams by collaborating, negotiating, and brainstorming to meet demands.

CHAPTER 7

Futuristic Artificial Intelligence

Purpose

- This chapter looks at the future trends of artificial intelligence (AI), risk, and security in 5 to 10 years.
- The good, bad, and ugly side of AI and machine learning (ML).
- How risk and security relates to AI and ML.

Chapter Outline

- Prediction of AI and ML and how they surpass human intelligence
- The negative side of AI to employment opportunities

Key Learning Points

- Learn and understand AI and where it is heading with intelligence

Possible Future

What is the future of AI in 5 or 10 years?

Currently, technology forecasters do not believe that human intelligence is likely to be surpassed (Yang and Yu 2019). Advances in AI will likely result in general reasoning systems and lack human cognitive limitations.

Some believe that AI and ML algorithms will eventually behave like humans and do the things humans do today. Currently, AI and ML keep track of consumer habits and respond accurately on selling to human consumers. Technology can change the way humans interact with their immediate surroundings.

We can ask ourselves questions today about the things that humans could not do 10 years back. The same questions can be asked about what humans can accomplish. In short, there will be some improvements and accomplishments in our lives.

Increase Security

Drones did not exist in the 1990s and phones were not easily available and attractive as they are now (Nassi et al. 2019). Drones can be perceived similarly to phones. Drones have numerous capabilities, such as transporting things through the air in a short period of time and to remote locations. Items that can be transported include package delivery and emergency response products to meet urgent and immediate needs. Drones can fly and inspect obscure places that are not easily accessible. Drones can be packed with AI features to make them intelligent.

Generate New Social Issues

AI is an extension of our abilities to solve problems and to provide new ideas to help humanity. It is possible for great things to come from AI, including advancement at an unprecedented rate. Assimilation of robots and AI in business operations can foresee AI-based products and services that will lead to consumer and industrial markets. The consumer and market areas will vary based on the innovators and business interests. AI will have challenges, such as cybersecurity issues. Organizations must fight the bad sides of AI, such as challenges with privacy, security, and algorithmic bias. The military, air force, and the navy will take interested in protecting countries from negative AI innovations.

Vesting Into Business and Health

AI- and ML-powered algorithms related to consumer applications may increase in confidence. This confidence and trust will increase the longer AI exists. This is all good!

Certainly, doctors are going to be around to take care of patients; however, the busy work of doctors can be done using AI. Doctors' knowledge and experience can be captured and used tirelessly by AI systems. Doctors will retire and AI systems will give doctors the break needed to retire. AI systems can maintain the most recent innovations, research, and experiences needed for patient care. AI can access and use a larger dataset of patient's data, treatment techniques, and advancements in medication. Diagnostic outcomes will improve when machines do the busy work for the doctor.

Facilitate Sustainability

AI is growing quickly and will impact every industry. More people are talking about AI; AI is not a new buzz phrase anymore. AI can improve the density of cities by tracking the movement of residents within cities.

Physical and Digital Coming Together

People have expressed the need for computers to react more intelligently with humans. A typical example is a computer pointing at errors that occur and automatically reacting to resolve the problem. Another option is to talk to the computer to fix issues that occur. In a nutshell, computers need to be smarter and AI can make it happen.

AI Is Going to Make Humans Smarter

The trend of AI and ML using formulae is going to continue and it is possible more algorithms will emerge (Metcalf et al. 2019; Ford 2019). It will not be a surprise when the amount of data increases exponentially. AI and ML will make intelligent projections on future behaviors and subsequent events by training more intelligent models and knowledge models. People in the financial environment are likely to get scared because of decisions AI and ML will be making. It is important that the models are trained appropriately to continue to grow as useful tools for humans.

What Does the Artist Gain From AI?

Artists would like to have a stake in AI to make artists' work easier and more fun (Miller, 2019). Artists will use numerous algorithms that will emerge exponentially. Hopefully, the artist can use AI systems to create beautiful images that are fun to look at. Artists may fear that their job will be taken over and make them obsolete. This is a frightening thought; however, the artist can use AI systems to become more creative in every sense. AI can augment the creative process. It is important to factor a sense of civility, creativity, and equity when deploying AI systems. Eventually, industries that use art can use AI to increase productivity while giving respect to human dignity and cultural needs.

Human Like AI

In 5 to 10 years of AI, it is believed that AI will begin to show human-like intelligence that includes the cognitive abilities of humans (Joo et al. 2019). Computers are already good at repetitive tasks, but this is not the same as having cognitive ability. Artificial general intelligence (AGI) seems to be emerging slowly. AI is currently used in technologies such as Uber and e-mail. Gmail tends to provide some initial e-mail responses that the user can build on.

AI has been used in hospitals to identify diseases in patients that human doctors have missed. This is encouraging to the patients; however, this example is classified as weak AI and referred to as AGI. AGI is simply a machine that can perform normal, human tasks. The current goal in AI is to develop a machine that must prove it is intelligent and distinguishable from a human.

Survey on AI Prediction

Participants of the 2019 Joint Multi-Conference on Human-Level Artificial Intelligence conducted a survey on the predictions of AI progress over the next 10 years (Strickland 2019). The outcome of the survey indicated that 28 percent of respondents believe that AGI will emerge within 20 years. Out of the 100 percent respondents, 2 percent do not believe that humans will see AGI.

The survey asked the respondents to indicate sectors where AI will have the greatest impact. The result showed the following:

(a) Health care (46 percent).
(b) Logistics (47 percent).
(c) Customer service (38 percent).
(d) Banking and finance (34 percent).
(e) Agriculture, retail, software development, and manufacturing (28 percent).

The survey indicated that AI is progressing exponentially.

An earlier survey on AI conducted in 2016 showed an outcome with less exciting results. The survey asked, "How many years before AI could pass high-level machine intelligence?" High-level machine intelligence is defined as unaided machines that accomplish tasks better and more cheaply than human workers. The end analysis showed five percent intervals for achieving AI milestones. The concrete outcome indicates that AI machines will eventually be competitive with human intelligence.

Risk and Security Effects of AI

AI falls into two domains of significant importance: employment and security. The increase of AI is due to cybersecurity, justice (criminal and civil), and labor market patterns. Furthermore, occupations are susceptible to automation.

How AI for Risk and Security Is Going to Shape Up?

Risk and security issues will exist with any task or project. These issues will increase as AI is used more in the future. The thought of AI making decisions worries some people; however, with training and education, humans will accept the reality of AI making decisions in different areas.

The following are some predicted and fictional ideas that may emerge in the future.

Finance Industry Sector

We can further include new technologies such as Bitcoin. Can Bitcoin become actual currency? This question leads to intense infrastructure planning to safeguard everyone's security fears. The security and risk associated with this helps protect against hackers.

Everything may become digital currency. The corporation that has a good communication network and access through Internet of Things (IoT) or connected devices to Cloud server environments will manage financial businesses. IoT data are currently being collected heavily in the business world. This has created opportunities for data analytics and for big data engineers and teams to purposefully deal with the collected data.

Retail Industry Sector

Retail stores may not require humans; anyone could pick up products from any store and directly charge to Bitcoin.

Automatic checkout would be used and make recommendations to the customer. Items would be available instantly through all connected devices. A person's home fridge would maintain a minimum quantity that is instantly delivered to a person's home based on the optimal quantity.

Humans need to find a way to earn money, and Bitcoin should be available to use for payment. Humans may own multiple specialized devices to serve customer needs such as purified water, a robot to prepare personalized foods, or a robot doctor that provides health advice.

Government Sector

Some may wonder what will happen to tax collections. The government may adopt automatic dynamic taxes instead of a fixed income tax. This method would require a political mandate to pass through congress.

Transportation Industry Sector

Driverless cars, driverless trucks, and drones for carrying goods and delivering to customers are determined by the user or owner of the drone.

Numerous risk and security issues will arise with the prediction provided earlier. Well-planned security and risk management will make this prediction feasible and humans will be able to enjoy the privileges that come with it.

Risk and security experts should be available to carry out adequate strategies that are testable in respective environments.

CHAPTER 8

Conclusion

Artificial Intelligence (AI) is becoming a phrase everywhere these days. You hear about AI on the television, radio, and the Internet. Risk and security has been a topic in everyone's mind, and security issues hurt organizations and individuals in the corporate world as well as domestically. Let us recap important reminders that will benefit all walks of life.

Risk and security issues are not fun to experience. Organizations do not take these predicaments lightly and often discuss the negative impact that is created. Do not turn your face away from risk and security; the negative impacts that come with them are not fun. Natural risk and security issues may unavoidable, but mitigations can be taken to save lives. Pay careful attention to follow the steps that are available.

Risks and security issues should be identified early to minimize the impact of damages or fatal situations. Risks usually require risk management to safely manage the situation. The data must be collected well; this will help when moving forward. This may require going through checklists to ensure that appropriate questions are answered, and appropriate steps are taken. This may also include capturing historical data on both risk and security issues. The next step is to analyze accurate data carefully and accurately. The captured data may help predict the future occurrence of risk and security issues. This approach may help salvage nasty situations that can be damaging and expensive to the individual or organization.

It is important to remember that there are hybrid types of security issues that an individual or organization must deal with. Careful analysis will provide accurate direction. AI has been chosen to provide the direction. The source of the data and quality of the data are crucial in every way. The content of the book has provided various use cases that organizations can relate to. The use cases will help organizations properly strategize the route to take. This leads to organizations defining, analyzing, monitoring, controlling, and mitigating risks and security.

Data science, data analytics, and machine learning (ML) algorithms are used to analyze the data and determine corrective actions. AI can be used to carry out all the necessary determinations. Machines can learn from previous human experiences as data input and enable continuous learning from new sets of input data based on the development of mathematical algorithms. Complete AI system development uses data collection to show how risk and security data are processed with recommendations. The data collection and development offer the reader an understanding of how to tackle use cases such as AI, risk, and security in an organization. AI is producing effective and dramatic results with businesses and with organizations that desire to understand and improve risk management skills.

Risk and security have become important everywhere due to the large volume of data, different velocity, and variety of data stemming from various sources, which is illustrated and supported with case studies. Risk and security concerns appear to be growing bigger and more frequent with any amount of negative impact. An undetermined positive risk can hurt organizations when it comes to business opportunities, leading to loss of revenue. The range and breadth of risk creates havoc everywhere in the world, and on a variety of projects. Risk and security can be devastating without appropriate management and the correct tools.

A lot of effort is focused on problem statements with appropriate use cases and proposals of AI solutions using data science and ML approaches. The comprehensive description of AI, risk, and security provides concrete answers to crucial questions that many organizations are struggling with: These questions are as follows: Where are these risks and what can be done to lower the impacts? Is AI part of the answers to security mitigations? Using AI, organizations and individuals will gain knowledge and shared experiences.

This book will guide organizations that are willing to create their own AI systems for risk and security. Additionally, Bizstats.ai has numerous customized AI design tools. Individuals and organizations are welcome to contact Bizstats.ai for training on the tools used in the implementation of the AI, risk, and security.

References

Alvarez-Ayllon, A., M. Palomo-Duarte, and D. Juan-Manuel. 2018. "Interactive Data Exploration of Distributed Raw Files: A Systematic Mapping Study." *IEEE Access* 7, 10691–10717. doi: https://doi.org/10.1109/ACCESS.2018.2882244

Andriosopoulos, D., M. Doumpos, P.M. Pardalos, and C. Zopounidis. 2019. "Computational Approaches and Data Analytics in Financial Services: A Literature Review." *Journal of the Operational Research Society* 70, no. 10, 1581. doi: https://doi.org/10.1080/01605682.2019.1595193

Aydos, M., Y. Vural, and A. Tekerek. 2019. "Assessing Risks and Threats with Layered Approach to Internet of Things Security." *Measurement & Control* 52, nos. 5/6, 338. doi: https://doi.org/10.1177/0020294019837991

Elswick, S.E., eds. 2016. *Data Collection: Methods, Ethical Issues and Future Directions.* Nova Science.

Ford, M. 2019. "The Truth Behind AI: Accelerating Tech—Insights from the Smarter Factory." *SMT: Surface Mount Technology* 34, no. 2, 60–66. http://iconnect007.uberflip.com/i/1078362-smt007-feb2019/59?m4=

Gheuens, J., N. Nagabhatla, and E.D.P. Perera. 2019. "Disaster-Risk, Water Security Challenges and Strategies in Small Island Developing States (SIDS)." *Water* 11, no. 4, 637. doi: https://doi.org/10.3390/w11040637

Gupta, G., and R. Katarya. June 14–15, 2018. "A Study of Recommender Systems Using Markov Decision Process." Paper presented at Second International Conference on Intelligent Computing and Control Systems (ICICCS). doi: https://doi.org 10.1109/ICCONS.2018.8663161

Haas, S., R. Conway-Phillips, B.A. Swan, L. De La Pena, R. Start, and D.S. Brown. 2019. "Developing a Business Case for the Care Coordination and Transition Management Model: Need, Methods, and Measures." *Nursing Economics* 37, no. 3, pp. 118–125.

Hill, M.S., G.W. Ruch, and G.K. Taylor. 2019. "Research and Development Expense and Analyst Forecast Errors: An Underestimation of Sales or Overestimation of Expenses?" *Journal of Accounting, Auditing & Finance* 34, no. 4, 667. doi: https://doi.org/10.1177/0148558X18799003

Huang, G., Z. Zhang, and W. Yang. 2019. "Outlier Detection Method based on Improved Two-step Clustering Algorithm and Synthetic Hypothesis Testing." Paper presented at the IEEE 8th Joint International Information Technology and Artificial Intelligence Conference (ITAIC). doi: https://doi.org/10.1109/ITAIC.2019.8785425

Jain, A., N.S. Bhandari, and N. Jain. February 21–23, 2018. "Essential Elements of Writing a Research/Review Paper for Conference/Journals." Paper presented at the 5th International Symposium on Emerging Trends and Technologies in Libraries and Information Services (ETTLIS). doi: 10.1109/ETTLIS.2018.8485210.

Joo, S.H., S. Manzoor, Y.G. Rocha, H.U. Lee, and T.Y. Kuc. 2019. "A Realtime Autonomous Robot Navigation Framework for Human Like High-Level Interaction and Task Planning in Global Dynamic Environment." Retrieved from the Cornell University website. https://arxiv.org/abs/1905.12942

Kotenko, I., I. Saenko, A. Kushnerevich, and A. Branitskiy. 2019. "Attack Detection in IoT Critical Infrastructures: A Machine Learning and Big Data Processing Approach." Paper presented at the 27th Euromicro International Conference on Parallel, Distributed and Network-Based Processing (PDP). doi: https://doi.org/10.1109/EMPDP.2019.8671571

Liu, Y., J. Dong, D. Zuo, and H. Liu. 2019. "Experimental Analysis and Comparison of Load Prediction Algorithms in Cloud Data Center." Presented at the IEEE 19th International Conference on Software Quality, Reliability and Security (QRS). doi: https://doi.org/10.1109/QRS.2019.00036

Mcgraw, G., R. Bonett, H. Figueroa, and V. Shepardson. 2019. "Security Engineering for Machine Learning." *Computer* 52, no. 8, 54. doi: https://doi.org/10.1109/MC.2019.2909955

Metcalf, L., D.A. Askay, and L.B. Rosenberg. 2019. "Keeping Humans in the Loop: Pooling Knowledge Through Artificial Swarm Intelligence to Improve Business Decision Making." *California Management Review* 61, no. 4, pp. 84–109. doi: https://doi.org/10.1177/0008125619862256

Miller, A. 2019. *The Artist in the Machine: The World of AI-Powered Creativity.* MIT Press.

Morosan, C., and A. DeFranco. 2019. "Classification and Characterization of U.S. Consumers Based on their Perceptions of Risk of Tablet Use in International Hotels: A Latent Profile Analysis." *Journal of Hospitality & Tourism Technology* 10, no. 11, 264. doi: https://doi.org/10.1108/jhtt-07-2018-0049

Nassi, B., A. Shabtai, R. Masuoka, and Y. Elovici. 2019. "SoK—Security and Privacy in the Age of Drones: Threats, Challenges, Solution Mechanisms, and Scientific Gaps." Retrieved from Cornell University website. https://arxiv.org/pdf/1903.05155.pdf

Ohanian, T. 2019. "How Artificial Intelligence and Machine Learning May Eventually Change Content Creation Methodologies." *SMPTE Motion Imaging Journal* 128, no. 1, 33–40. doi: https://doi.org/10.5594/JMI.2018.2876781

Overgoor, G., M. Chica, W. Rand, and A. Weishampel. 2019. "Letting the Computers Take Over: Using AI to Solve Marketing Problems." *California Management Review* 61, no. 4, 156–185. doi: https://doi.org/10.1177/0008125619859318

Palli, R., M.G. Palshikar, and J. Thakar. 2019. "Executable Pathway Analysis Using Ensemble Discrete-State Modeling for Large-Scale Data." *PLoS Computational Biology* 15, no. 9, 1–21. doi: https://doi.org/10.1371/journal.pcbi.1007317

Peters, K. 2018. "Disasters, Climate Change, and Securitisation: The United Nations Security Council and the United Kingdom's Security Policy." *Disasters* 42, no. S2, S196–S214. doi: https://doi.org/10.1111/disa.12307

Phillips, P.P., and C.A. Stawarski. 2008. *Data Collection: Planning for and Collecting All Types of Data*. Pfeiffer.

Rona-Tas, A., A. Cornuéjols, S. Blanchemanche, A. Duroy, and C. Martin. 2019. "Enlisting Supervised Machine Learning in Mapping Scientific Uncertainty Expressed in Food Risk Analysis." *Sociological Methods & Research* 48, no. 3, 608–641. doi: https://doi.org/10.1177/0049124117729701

Sahoo, P. and J.R. Mohanty. 2018. "Test Effort Estimation in Early Stages Using Use Case and Class Models for Web Applications." *International Journal of Knowledge Based Intelligent Engineering Systems* 22, no. 3, 215–229. doi: https://doi.org/10.3233/KES-180386

Samson, R.M. 2010. *Supply-Chain Management: Theories, Activities/Functions, and Problems*. Nova Science.

Shrestha, Y.R., S.M. Ben-Menahem, and G. von Krogh. 2019. "Organizational Decision-Making Structures in the Age of Artificial Intelligence." *California Management Review* 61, no. 4, 66–83. doi: https://doi.org/10.1177/0008125619862257

Strickland, E. 2019. "How Smart is Artificial Intelligence? Are Today's Best Artificial-Intelligence Systems as Smart as a Mouse? A Crow? A Chimp? A New Contest Aims to Find Out." *IEEE Spectrum* 56, no. 4. doi: https://doi.org/10.1109/MSPEC.2019.8678419

Sutton, R.S., and A.G. Barto. 1998. *Reinforcement Learning: An Introduction*. Bradford Book.

Vaez-Alaei, M., A. Baboli, and R. Tavakkoli-Moghaddam. 2018. "A New Approach to Integrate Resilience Engineering and Business Process Reengineering Design." Paper presented at the IEEE International Conference on Industrial Engineering and Engineering Management (IEEM). doi: https://doi.org/10.1109/IEEM.2018.8607662

Wang, J., S. Hazarika, C. Li, and H. Shen. 2019. "Visualization and Visual Analysis of Ensemble Data: A Survey." Paper presented at IEEE Transactions on Visualization and Computer Graphics, Visualization and Computer Graphics. doi: https://doi.org/10.1109/TVCG.2018.2853721

Yang, X., and X. Yu. March 2–4, 2019. "Identifying Patent Risks in Technological Competition: A Patent Analysis of Artificial Intelligence Industry." Paper presented at the 8th International Conference on Industrial Technology and Management (ICITM). doi: https://doi.org/10.1109/ICITM.2019.8710719

About the Authors

Archie Addo is a consultant, coach, author, and program and project manager. Archie holds a PhD in computer information systems with an emphasis in e-commerce, cryptography, expert systems, and artificial intelligence. Dr. Addo has an executive data science certification from Johns Hopkins University and a certificate in Contract Law from Harvard Law School. He is a Certified Project Management Professional, Certified ScrumMaster, and a Certified Scrum Product Owner. With more than 20 years of experience in interrelated disciplines, Archie works with computer science, project management, procurement, organizational design and development, process engineering, quality management, and project team facilitation. He has held management positions including software development, manager, consultant, and senior project manager.

Archie is a subject matter expert reviewer for global congress and the India Congress Project Management Institute and is a contributor to PMI Risk Standard Management.

Srini Centhala is the founder and chief architect of Absolut-e Data Com (a data company) that had provided expert consulting services to Fortune 100 companies such AT&T, Directv, Experian, eBay, and UPS for more than 20 years. Srini is also the chief architect of BizStats Cloud Big Data AI Analytics platform. Srini has designed and developed pricing engines, statistical modeling, prediction modeling, recommendation engine, text mining, sentiment analysis, data source analysis, and data science activities.

Specialties: Business process re-engineering, online business ideas, and concepts, business intelligence, technical architect/data architect/data modeler in the business data management system, project management, and undertaking full projects, end to end. Srini applies machine learning and artificial intelligence to business data.

Muthu Shanmugam is the chief technology officer at Absolut-e Data Com with more than 20 years of experience in all phases of the software development life cycle. Muthu holds a master of engineering from Anna University, India. He has worked with various enterprise organizations as a dynamic leader of software development teams. Currently, Muthu works on Bizstats.ai, a knowledge-base-powered business intelligence and analytics cloud designed for businesses with limited business intelligence resources. Key features include knowledge bases with numerous metrics and attributes for various industries, natural language processing-powered searches, dynamic reports, and dashboards. The company also features collaboration, which allows users to share reports and dashboards with their teams.

Index

**OTHER TITLES IN THE BUSINESS LAW AND
CORPORATE RISK MANAGEMENT COLLECTION**

John Wood, Econautics Sustainability Institute, Editors

- *Preventing Litigation* by Nelson E. Brestoff and William H. Inmon
- *Buyer Beware* by Elvira Medici and Linda J. Spievack
- *Corporate Maturity and the "Authentic Company"* by David Jackman
- *Light on Peacemaking* by Thomas DiGrazia
- *Cybersecurity Law* by Shimon Brathwaite
- *Understanding Consumer Bankruptcy* by Scott B. Kuperberg

Announcing the Business Expert Press Digital Library

Concise e-books business students need for classroom and research

This book can also be purchased in an e-book collection by your library as

- a one-time purchase,
- that is owned forever,
- allows for simultaneous readers,
- has no restrictions on printing, and
- can be downloaded as PDFs from within the library community.

Our digital library collections are a great solution to beat the rising cost of textbooks. E-books can be loaded into their course management systems or onto students' e-book readers.
The **Business Expert Press** digital libraries are very affordable, with no obligation to buy in future years. For more information, please visit **www.businessexpertpress.com/librarians**. To set up a trial in the United States, please email **sales@businessexpertpress.com**.